The Argument Writing Toolkit

In order for students to *write* effective arguments, they need to *read* good arguments. In this practical book, you'll find out how to use mentor texts to make writing instruction more meaningful, authentic, and successful. Author Sean Ruday demonstrates how you can teach middle school students to analyze the qualities of effective arguments and then help them think of those qualities as tools to improve their own writing. You'll learn how to:

- ♦ introduce high-interest topics to students to get them interested and engaged in argument writing;
- ♦ teach students to look at multiple sides of an issue and critically evaluate evidence to construct informed, defensible arguments;
- ♦ make argument writing an interactive, student-driven exercise in which students pursue their own writing projects;
- ♦ use mentor texts to help students learn the core concepts of argument writing and apply those skills across the curriculum.

The book is filled with examples and templates you can bring back to the classroom immediately, as well as an annotated bibliography which links the concepts in this book to the corresponding Common Core State Standards. Blank templates are also available as printable eResources on our website (www.routledge.com/9781138924390).

Sean Ruday is Assistant Professor of English Education at Longwood University. He is also the author of *The Informational Writing Toolkit*, *The Common Core Grammar Toolkit, Grades 6–8*, and *The Common Core Grammar Toolkit, Grades 3–5*.

The Argument Writing Toolkit

Using Mentor Texts in Grades 6–8

Sean Ruday

Routledge
Taylor & Francis Group

NEW YORK AND LONDON

First published 2016
by Routledge
711 Third Avenue, New York, NY 10017

and by Routledge
2 Park Square, Milton Park, Abingdon, Oxon, OX14 4RN

Routledge is an imprint of the Taylor & Francis Group, an informa business

Library of Congress Cataloging-in-Publication Data
Ruday, Sean.
  The argument writing toolkit : teaching argument writing in grades 6–8 / by Sean Ruday.
      pages cm
  Includes bibliographical references.
  1. English language—Composition and exercises—Study and teaching (Elementary) 2. English language—Composition and exercises—Study and teaching (Middle school) 3. Persuasion (Rhetoric)—Study and teaching (Elementary) 4. Persuasion (Rhetoric)—Study and teaching (Middle school) I. Title.
  LB1576.R775 2016
    428.0071'2—dc23
    2015007370

ISBN: 978-1-138-92437-6 (hbk)
ISBN: 978-1-138-92439-0 (pbk)
ISBN: 978-1-315-68440-6 (ebk)

Typeset in Palatino and Formata
by Apex Covantage, LLC

Contents

eResources

The appendices of this book can also be downloaded and printed for classroom use. You can access these downloads by visiting the book product page on our website: www.routledge.com/books/details/9781138924390. Then click on the tab that says "eResources," and select the files. They will begin downloading to your computer.

Meet the Author

Sean Ruday is an Assistant Professor of English Education at Longwood University. He began his teaching career at a public school in Brooklyn, NY, and has taught English and language arts in New York, Massachusetts, and Virginia. He holds a BA from Boston College, an MA from New York University, and a PhD from the University of Virginia. Sean is a Co-President of the Assembly for the Teaching of English Grammar—a grammar-focused affiliate of the National Council of Teachers of English. Some publications in which his articles have appeared are: *Journal of Teaching Writing, Journal of Language and Literacy Education, Contemporary Issues in Technology and Teacher Education*, and the *Yearbook of the Literacy Research Association*. He enjoys talking with teachers about innovative ways to improve students' literacy learning. His professional website is seanruday.weebly.com. You can follow him on Twitter @SeanRuday. This is his fourth book with Routledge Eye on Education.

Acknowledgments

I am thankful for all of the support and assistance I have received while writing this book. I greatly appreciate the middle school teachers who opened their classrooms to me, allowing me to work with their students. Similarly, I am grateful for the wonderful students in those classes who eagerly dove into the ideas and tools of argument writing. I would also like to thank the students whose writings are included in this book; I am thrilled to feature their works. I am very thankful for the guidance and support of this book's editor, Lauren Davis, who has been a wonderfully encouraging presence in my writing career. I am also thankful for my colleague, mentor, and friend, Derek Taylor, whose guidance has proved invaluable. I would like to thank my parents, Bob and Joyce Ruday, for all that they have done for me. I am beyond grateful for their love and support. I also want to thank my wife, Clare Ruday, who brightens my life by bringing humor and happiness to it.

Presenting the Tools of Argument Writing to Middle School Students

It's a chilly, overcast day, the kind that seems to be made for blankets and hot chocolate, but the cold temperatures and cloudy skies outside have not lessened the energy of the seventh grade students with whom I'm working. I'm consulting at these students' middle school, working with the students and teachers on the craft of argument writing. The objective for today's lesson is to use high-interest topics to get the students started thinking about effective arguments.

I begin the class with an inquiry: "From all of the books you've read," I say to the students, "which character struck you as the bravest?"

Student hands fly into the air. I call on specific individuals and record their responses on the whiteboard.

"It's definitely Katniss Everdeen from *The Hunger Games*," asserts a young lady. "She's incredibly brave! She volunteered as tribute in place of her sister, and did so many other things too!"

"I think Harry Potter is the bravest from all the books I've read," replies another student. "Especially the way he fought Voldemort. That was brave!"

Another student exclaims, "I think it's gotta be Charlotte Doyle" (from the book *The True Confessions of Charlotte Doyle* by Avi). "She did a bunch of things that scared her while she was traveling on a ship without her family, but she still did them. She earned the respect of the crew because of the bravery she showed."

"Great job, all of you," I respond. "So far, we have Katniss Everdeen, Harry Potter, and Charlotte Doyle. I want to stop for a second and call attention to something great that our volunteers did: each one stated a claim and supported that claim with specific evidence. These are both important parts of creating an effective argument; if you're going to argue for something, you need to tell people what you're arguing in favor of and support that statement with evidence. These things I just mentioned are two of the tools of effective arguments. In the next several classes, we're going to talk about argument writing. While we do this, we'll discuss a whole bunch of tools that strong argument writers use to make their works as effective as possible. Once you know all of these tools, you'll be able to write an awesome argumentative essay on anything you want—such as an essay arguing that Katniss Everdeen, Harry Potter, or Charlotte Doyle is especially brave. Sound good?" The students nod their heads and I smile, excited by their interest in mastering the tools of argument writing.

This excerpt from my conversation with these seventh graders is an example of the ideas and instructional methods described in this book. I wrote this book to provide a resource for middle school teachers interested in ideas, activities, and strategies that can help their students master argument writing. Given the emphasis the Common Core State Standards (2010) and other rigorous state standards place on argument writing, it's no surprise to me that many of the pre-service and in-service teachers with whom I work have asked for resources and support related to teaching this genre. I recently spoke with a novice teacher named Kate, who was in her first year of teaching middle school English and looking for extra support regarding teaching argument writing: "I know argument writing is important," she explained, "and not just for the Common Core, but also for our students' futures. The problem is, I really need help getting my students to see the difference between a strong argument and a weak one. I'm struggling with coming up with ways to teach them what a strong argument is and why it's strong." The concerns Kate expresses are important ones; as teachers of argument writing, we must help our students understand the attributes of strong arguments and then enable them to apply these characteristics to their own works.

This book seeks to meet the needs of teachers like Kate who want to understand the best ways to teach argument writing to middle school students. It addresses the following essential questions: 1) What are the attributes of effective argument writing?, and 2) What are the best ways to help middle school students understand those attributes and apply them to their own argument writing? It provides explanations, examples, and recommendations to use when teaching your students about effective argument writing. This introductory chapter is divided into the following sections, each of which addresses a key element of this book's approach to argument writing instruction:

- ◆ The importance of argument writing.
- ◆ The toolkit metaphor.
- ◆ The significance of mentor texts.
- ◆ The gradual release of responsibility method of instruction.
- ◆ The unique needs of middle school writers.
- ◆ What to expect in this book, including the specific Common Core Writing Standards this book addresses.

The Importance of Argument Writing

While argument writing is an especially significant focus of the Common Core State Standards (CCSS), Barbara Moss (2014) explains that many middle school teachers don't yet feel very comfortable teaching it: "While many middle grade teachers feel comfortable teaching persuasion, far fewer feel the same level of comfort with teaching argument" (p. 61). Although the Common Core's focus on argument writing represents a challenging instructional shift in many middle school classrooms, research strongly indicates the benefits of teaching our students the tools of effective argument writing (Hillocks, 2010). The CCSS identify the ability to construct an effective argument as a key component of college- and career-readiness. This assertion makes a great deal of sense when one considers that students who study argument writing are able to: 1) Consider multiple sides of important issues, 2) Evaluate pieces of evidence, and 3) Develop strong understandings of logic. In this section, we'll examine each of these points individually.

Consider Multiple Sides of Important Issues

Considering multiple sides of important issues is a key component of effective argument writing. Many argumentative works that middle school students write address complex ideas and social issues; students that carefully consider both sides of an important issue not only create stronger works, but can also grow as writers and thinkers. First, let's examine the idea that acknowledging opposing ideas leads to strong argumentative pieces (Lunsford & Ruszkiewicz, 2012). Acknowledging alternative perspectives and refuting them can enhance the strength of one's argument; a seventh grader with whom I recently worked noted the significance of this strategy: "In my paper, I'm arguing that teachers should get paid more than they do. I think my paper's better now that I've discussed what people who don't think this might say. Discussing what those people might say shows I know what the other side thinks and gives me a chance to show that I still think those people are wrong."

In addition, acknowledging opposing claims helps students grow as writers and thinkers; students who write about nuanced social issues need to adequately consider alternative viewpoints in order to accurately capture the complex social issues associated with those issues. For example, I recently spoke with a seventh grade teacher who noted how much stronger his students' argumentative writings were after they incorporated opposing viewpoints into their works: "I have four students writing argument essays about gun control—two for and two against," he explained. "Before they acknowledged the opposing viewpoints to their positions and talked about them, all of their essays were really simplistic. Now that they've all also acknowledged the other sides, it's clearer that they've thought about these issues." This teacher also noted that some of his students had not yet fully considered alternate perspectives to their beliefs on certain issues: "I think a lot of [my students] learned more about their topics from reading about opposing viewpoints. I think some of them hadn't ever thought about the other side of their argument until we did this."

Evaluate Pieces of Evidence

Students who study argument writing also learn to critically evaluate pieces of evidence. Since a well-crafted argument employs strong evidence to support the author's point, it's crucial that students carefully evaluate pieces of evidence when deciding whether or not to include them in their works. Doing so helps students learn to differentiate between evidence that effectively supports their arguments and evidence that does not. For example, I recently worked with a sixth grader who noted how thinking critically about specific pieces of evidence helped her argue that standardized tests should be de-emphasized: "My essay argues that standardized tests shouldn't be so important. There are a bunch of ideas out there, but I wanted to make sure to use strong evidence from credible sources that enhances my argument. I used facts about not as many colleges requiring the SAT to show that it's okay for middle schools to not make standardized tests so important." This student's teacher also noted that teaching students to evaluate pieces of evidence enhanced their argumentative works: "My students are doing so much better on argument writing now that they're thinking carefully about what evidence they include. Before, they would just bring in any evidence. Now they're thinking about what we taught them: if that evidence actually supports their points and if it's from a reliable source." Thinking about these issues helps students evaluate information they encounter, improving their skills as argument writers as well as their overall critical thinking abilities.

Develop Strong Understandings of Logic

The study of argument writing also helps students develop strong understandings of logic, as it teaches students to closely examine information and formulate defensible arguments that emerge from it (Hillocks, 2010). Hillocks explains that a key difference between persuasive and argument writing is that argument writing heavily emphasizes logical thinking, while persuasive writing often does not. According to Hillocks, an effective argument begins with the examination of data—once a writer has considered the relevant data surrounding a topic, she or he can create an argument that is rooted in this information. This contributes to students' abilities to introduce logical claims and support them with evidence, skills that are required by the Common Core Standards and described in detail in this book.

In this book, we'll examine a number of specific ways to help students think carefully about the arguments they construct—a skill that, given the Common Core's statement that creating and defending arguments is crucial to students' college- and career-readiness, will continue to pay dividends for our students throughout their lives. The argument writing strategies we'll explore in this text can be applied across the curriculum; while argument writing is important to middle school English instruction, it is also an essential concept in science and social studies classes. Fisher and Frey (2013) advocate for students to write in all subject areas to enhance their writing skills as well as their knowledge of these subjects. Many of the examples described in this book address issues that are relevant to multiple subject areas and can be used as models for students as they write across the curriculum, such as an essay in Appendix A about the importance of gym class to students' academic performance or a student's piece about the merits of hybrid cars. In addition, the writing strategies I discuss in this book transcend subject areas and can be applied to argument writing in any academic discipline.

The Toolkit Metaphor

Now that we've examined the importance of argument writing and the benefits associated with it, let's think about the toolkit metaphor, a central concept in this book. In this book, I explain that the writing strategies effective argument writers use are like tools that craftspeople use to achieve certain tasks. I describe the Common Core Standards of argument writing as tools that strong writers use with specific goals in mind. In order to properly apply one of these writing tools, an author must think carefully about what particular result she or he wants to achieve. A craftsperson would use a hammer in one instance and a drill in another, just as an argument writer would focus on acknowledging opposing claims in one situation and composing a concluding section in a different one. All of these writing strategies are specific tools that argument writers use in specific instances to make their works as effective as possible.

In this book, we'll examine a wide range of tools of argument writing. Each of these tools will add to your students' abilities to meet the Common Core Standards by crafting effective arguments. I recently spoke with a group of middle school teachers about the toolkit metaphor, explaining to them that each one of the writing strategies that comprise effective argument writing represents a specific tool their students need to have in their writing toolkits. One teacher in this group captured the toolkit metaphor perfectly: "I love this [approach to writing instruction] because it shows students all of the different skills they've mastered. Once they've mastered a skill, they can add it to their toolkits. My eighth graders love collecting stuff—video games, shoes, jerseys—and collecting skills for their argument writing toolkits is totally something they'll get."

This teacher's comment is exemplary for a number of reasons: not only does it show a great awareness of her students' interests, but it also speaks to the importance of students' metacognitive awareness of particular writing strategies. Metacognition—students' knowledge of cognitive phenomena (Flavell, 1979)—is an important component of effective writing instruction and central to the toolkit approach. As students learn about specific writing strategies and add those strategies to their toolkits, they enhance their metacognitive awareness of the components of effective writing. The more strategies the students understand, the more effective writers they can become. As I'll explain in this book, students' awareness of the tools of argument writing is crucial to their abilities to create strong argumentative pieces. The strategies in our students' toolkits—and their understandings of how to use them—are directly related to their successes as writers.

The Significance of Mentor Texts

In order for our students to understand the tools of effective argument writing, we teachers must first show them especially effective examples of strong argumentative works. These examples, frequently called mentor texts, provide students with concrete models of how to use specific writing strategies in their own works. The primary goal of a mentor text is to add to students' abilities to be effective writers by showing them something that an effective writer does in his or her work (Ray, 1999). Once we show students these examples, we can talk with them about how to apply these same strategies to their own pieces.

While many effective authors learn about the craft of writing through reading and imitating (Killgallon & Killgallon, 2013), mentor texts are not always used as frequently as they could be. A seventh grade school teacher told me that his students had not seen mentor examples used to teach effective writing strategies in their previous years of schooling: "My students said that, in earlier grades, they were given outlines and worksheets to help them write. They said this is the first time they're learning about writing by looking at what other writers do. They're really enjoying it."

In this book, we'll examine how to use mentor texts to teach students the tools of effective argument writing. Each chapter in the book contains mentor examples that illustrate the use of the writing strategy that the chapter addresses. These examples are taken from the argument essays in Appendix A, which contains complete versions of the essays featured in this book. The essays in this appendix are mentor texts I wrote to show my middle school students the tools of effective argument writing. In each chapter, I refer to specific excerpts from these essays that represent the chapter's concept and describe how those excerpts can be used to help students understand that particular aspect of effective argument writing. For example, in Chapter 4, which focuses on the argument writing strategy of organizing reasons and evidence logically, I refer to the mentor text "Smaller Classes, Successful Students," found in Appendix A. I call attention to the organization of reasons and evidence in this essay, describe why the essay is effective in this way, and describe how this example can be used to help students apply this strategy to their own argumentative pieces.

The Gradual Release of Responsibility Method of Instruction

Middle schoolers are not known to be a passive bunch! Many middle school teachers with whom I've spoken have commented on the constant energy that fills the halls and classrooms of their schools. In fact, today's middle school students explain that they learn much better in an active classroom than in one in which they are "passive audience members" (Steinberg & McCray, 2012, p. 7). Fortunately, there is a way to teach students effectively while also ensuring they are actively involved in the learning process: the gradual release of responsibility method of instruction (Pearson & Gallagher, 1983). This instructional process consists of three key components. First, teachers use a mini-lesson to explain a specific concept to students, providing descriptions and examples to ensure the students clearly understand. At this point in the process, teachers take on the majority of the responsibility; the students have more of a passive role. Second, teachers work with students on the concept by engaging them in interactive activities, answering questions, and evaluating their understandings. In this stage, more of the responsibility for the students' learning is shared between the teacher and students. Finally, students work on a concept independently—through an activity like creating their own pieces of writing and applying the lesson's focal strategy to those pieces—while teachers check with them individually and provide them with one-on-one feedback. In this final stage, the students take on the majority of the learning responsibility.

While the gradual release of responsibility method can be applied to a variety of subjects, it is an especially effective method of writing instruction (Fisher & Frey, 2003). Fletcher and Portalupi (2001) explain that this method of instruction actively engages students in ways that other forms of writing instruction do not, allowing students to take ownership of their writing in the form of an apprenticeship model that varies from traditional (and more passive) writing instruction. The instructional recommendations described in this book follow the gradual release of responsibility method, providing specific suggestions for explaining the tools of argument writing to your students, working with students as they become more familiar with these tools, and then ultimately "turning the students loose" while they apply these strategies (and supporting them as they do so). As you read these recommendations, you'll develop a strong understanding of how to make your students active and engaged students of argument writing.

The Needs of Middle School Writers

Since this book focuses specifically on teaching the tools of argument writing to middle school students, it's important to acknowledge some especially significant needs and attributes of middle school writers. In this section, I address the following characteristics of middle school writers: 1) Middle school students want to explore high-interest topics, 2) Middle school students want to write for audiences other than their teachers, and 3) Middle school students learn best from strategies and examples, not from formulas. Let's explore each of these characteristics in detail.

Middle School Students Want to Explore High-Interest Topics

Middle school students want to assert their individual identities (Steinberg & McCray, 2012), which, in the context of writing, often means exploring high-interest topics that they personally value, such as issues that are relevant to their lives and communities. However, writing instruction in today's schools frequently focuses on mandatory prompts and test-prep programs (NCTE, 2008). Middle-school-writing experts such as Laura Robb (2010) and Nancie Atwell (1998) urge teachers to help their students write about high-interest, relevant topics instead of mandated, test-prep ones, and with good reason: adolescents who explore high-interest topics in their English classes are motivated by the chance to become experts on subjects important to themselves and their peers (Knoester, 2009). Let's apply this idea specifically to argument writing: if students are able to examine information about issues that matter to them and construct arguments about these topics, it stands to reason that they will be much more motivated to investigate those issues and formulate effective arguments about them than if they were working with mandatory topics without that same relevance.

Middle School Students Want to Write for Audiences Other than Their Teachers

The importance of high-interest topics described in the preceding paragraph relates to the idea that middle school students want to write for audiences other than their teachers. The presence of a strong writing community is an important motivating factor in adolescents' desires to write (Abbott, 2000). Robb (2010) explains that middle schoolers often enjoy the interactive nature of blogging, as it provides opportunities for students to read, comment on, and learn from one another. In today's social-media and information-communication-technology-rich environment, middle schoolers frequently write to communicate. In the writing classroom, we can capitalize on this trend by helping students write for broader audiences than their teachers. By using blogs, publishing celebrations, and other forms of collaboration, we can take advantage of students' desires to write for authentic and meaningful audiences. In this book, we'll explore specific instances in which students craft argumentative pieces for wide audiences, such as the student we'll meet in Chapter 3 who used a blog to share his argument that young baseball players need to change the ways they play in order to prevent arm injuries when they are older.

Middle School Students Learn Best from Strategies and Examples, Not from Formulas

While a great deal of writing instruction in today's middle schools uses formulas, scripts, and templates (Robb, 2010), research indicates that these "one size fits all" programs are not the best way to teach students to master the craft of writing (Graham & Perin, 2007). Instead, middle school writing instruction is most effective when teachers focus on specific writing strategies, providing students with understandings of what the strategies of effective writing are and helping them apply those strategies to their own works (Graham & Perin, 2007). In this book, we'll explore specific strategies, or tools, that facilitate effective argument writing. These tools will help your students meet the Common Core State Standards for argument writing and will help them become strong writers and thinkers who are well-positioned for high school, college, and their future careers.

What to Expect in This Book

This book identifies the tools that the Common Core Standards say middle school students need to be able to use in order to become effective argument writers, and discusses specific, classroom-ready practices to help students acquire these tools. This book is divided into three sections.

♦ Section 1, which focuses on argument writing strategies aligned with the Common Core Standards for Grades 6 through 8. Each of the seven chapters in this section addresses an important element of argument writing and explains how to help your students grasp that concept. For consistency and ease of use, I've organized each chapter in this section in the following format:
  ♦ An introduction to the chapter's focal concept. This opening section provides a description and some examples of the focal concept addressed in the chapter.
  ♦ A discussion of why the concept is important to strong argument writing. This section explains why authors use this particular concept when writing argumentative pieces and includes mentor examples from argumentative essays to illustrate how the concept looks in practice.
  ♦ A classroom snapshot. Each snapshot contains a description of my experiences teaching the chapter's focal concept to a sixth, seventh, or eighth grade class during my recent work at a middle school. I've included these snapshots so you can see how I taught my students about these important aspects of argument writing and learn from these concrete examples as you work with your own students.
  ♦ Specific instructional recommendations. Each chapter closes with specific recommendations for you to keep in mind when engaging your middle school students in learning activities that focus on these concepts.

- ◆ Section 2, which focuses on "Putting It Together." The first chapter in this section focuses on strategies and easy-to-follow rubrics to use when assessing your students' argument writing, while the next chapter addresses final thoughts and tips that will help you as you put the ideas and recommendations described in this book into practice in your own classroom.
- ◆ Section 3, which features the following resources designed to help you put this book's ideas into action:
  - ◆ Appendix A, which contains complete versions of the argument essays featured in this book. As previously mentioned, the essays in this appendix are mentor texts I wrote to show my middle school students the tools of effective argument writing.
  - ◆ Appendix B, which contains reproducible charts and forms you can use in your classroom.
  - ◆ Appendix C, which contains information on helping your students select relevant and engaging argument writing topics.
  - ◆ An annotated bibliography, which includes excerpts from the argument essays featured in this book, the aspect of effective argument writing featured in each example, and the Common Core Standard associated with that concept.
  - ◆ The book's reference list.

Table I.1 lists the aspects of argument writing described in this book, the chapters in which they are discussed, and the Common Core Writing Standards with which each aligns.

TABLE I.1 Chapter Overview Table

Aspect of Argument Writing	Chapter	Related Common Core Writing Standards
Introducing claims	Chapter 1	W.6.1.A, W.7.1.A, W.8.1.A
Acknowledging alternate or opposing claims	Chapter 2	W.7.1.A, W.8.1.A
Supporting claims with reasons and evidence while using credible sources	Chapter 3	W.6.1.B, W.7.1.B, W.8.1.B
Organizing reasons and evidence logically	Chapter 4	W.6.1.A, W.7.1.A, W.8.1.A
Using words, phrases, and clauses to create cohesion and clarify relationships	Chapter 5	W.6.1.C, W.7.1.C, W.8.1.C
Establishing and maintaining a formal style	Chapter 6	W.6.1.D, W.7.1.D, W.8.1.D
Creating an effective concluding section	Chapter 7	W.6.1.E, W.7.1.E, W.8.1.E

Teaching the strategies of argument writing to middle schoolers isn't easy, but it's extremely important to their college- and career-readiness, as well as their abilities to be informed and thoughtful members of society. This book will give you practical and useful information you can use to help your middle school students master this genre. In the book, we'll look together at the key components of effective argument writing, what exactly those components are, why they are important, how they are used in mentor examples of argument writing, and specific ways to put them into practice in your classroom. My goal is for you to finish this book and say, "I know all about the tools of argument writing and I'm ready to help my middle school students learn them through engaging and effective methods." If you're ready to learn how to do this, then keep reading!

Section 1

Argument Writing Strategies Aligned with the Common Core Standards for Grades 6–8

1

Introducing Claims

What Does "Introducing Claims" Mean?

A fundamental component of effective argument writing is introducing the claim for which the author is arguing. For example, the students mentioned in the vignette at the beginning of this book's introduction stated their individual claims for the bravest book character (recall that one student claimed Katniss Everdeen was the bravest, another said Harry Potter, and a third supported Charlotte Doyle). The Common Core State Standards highlight the importance of this concept, as Standards W.6.1.A, W.7.1.A, and W.8.1.A emphasize the importance of effectively introducing claims in argument writing. In this chapter, we'll discuss the following: what "introducing claims" means, why this concept is important for effective argument writing, a description of a lesson on this concept, and key recommendations for helping your students effectively introduce claims in their own argument writing. Along the way, we'll take a look at examples of argument writing and explore how the claims in those examples are introduced.

Let's begin by examining what it means to introduce a claim. Authors of argument writing need to begin by clearly telling their readers what they are going to be arguing in that piece—they do this by introducing the piece's claim. When introducing a piece's claim, the author doesn't yet describe the topic in depth—that comes later in the essay! Instead, he or she takes a position that will be further developed throughout the course of the essay. For example, the argument essay "Schools Should Stay Away from Computer Grading" introduces its claim in its opening paragraph, stating "Even though computer programs that grade student writing are gaining popularity, schools should stay away from them.

Computer grading does not provide students with important benefits that teacher grading does." This excerpt shows readers what the author will be arguing, but it doesn't yet go into a lot of detail. Instead, it tells readers that, as they continue with the essay, they'll learn more about why the author has taken this stance. In the next section of this chapter, we'll consider why clearly introducing a claim is important to argument writing.

Why Introducing a Claim Is Important to Effective Argument Writing

Introducing a claim is especially important to an effective piece of argument writing for two related reasons: 1) It provides a sense of focus by taking a side on an issue, and 2) It establishes a foundation for the rest of the piece. Without a clearly stated claim, an argument essay wouldn't take a position on an issue and wouldn't have a stance to support throughout the rest of the piece. If the first paragraph of the essay "Schools Should Stay Away from Computer Grading" didn't introduce its claim, it wouldn't provide the same sense of focus and wouldn't reveal what the rest of the piece is going to explain.

To further explore this, let's take a look at the opening paragraph of "Schools Should Stay Away from Computer Grading" and then examine how that paragraph would look without the section that introduces the piece's claim. The piece's full opening paragraph reads:

> How are computers used in your school? They might be used by students for typing papers, creating presentations, and doing research. They might be used by teachers for taking attendance, recording students' grades, and emailing administrators. A hot topic in education today is the idea that computer programs can grade students' writing. Software developers have recently created programs that can grade students' papers, creating a situation in which teachers no longer grade their students' works. These programs have been adopted in several colleges and even some middle and high schools. Even though computer programs that grade student writing are gaining popularity, schools should stay away from them. Computer grading does not provide students with important benefits that teacher grading does.

Notice that this paragraph introduces its claim in its final two sentences, saying "Even though computer programs that grade student writing are gaining popularity, schools should stay away from them. Computer grading does not provide students with important benefits that teacher grading does." These sentences give the essay a sense of focus, indicating that this essay will argue that schools should not use programs that grade student writing. This sense of focus also provides a foundation for the rest of the piece—as the essay continues, the author can keep developing this idea with reasons, evidence, and other information.

The text below illustrates how the opening paragraph of this essay would look without the sentences that introduce the piece's claim:

> How are computers used in your school? They might be used by students for typing papers, creating presentations, and doing research. They might be used by teachers for taking attendance, recording students' grades, and emailing administrators. A hot topic in education today is the idea that computer programs can grade students' writing. Software developers have recently created programs that can grade students' papers, creating a situation in which teachers no longer grade their students' works. These programs have been adopted in several colleges and even some middle and high schools.

Without the final two sentences that introduce the piece's claim, this paragraph reads much differently. It states some possible uses of computers in schools and introduces the idea of computer programs that can grade student writing, but does not take a side on this issue. In fact, without the claim-introducing section, this doesn't even appear to be taken from a piece of argument writing! This paragraph doesn't take a side on the issue and doesn't clearly communicate what the rest of the piece will be describing. If you read an essay that featured this opening paragraph, you might ask yourself, "What is the author going to tell me in this piece? Is he or she going to continue describing computer programs that grade student writing? Is he or she going to describe other ways computers are used in schools?" Without answers to these questions, it would be difficult to determine the goal of the essay. However, introducing a claim avoids this confusion; if this paragraph included a clear claim, readers could understand the author's purpose for writing the essay.

Let's continue to consider the importance of introducing a claim by examining another excerpt from an argument essay: the opening paragraph from the essay "Don't Trust Amazon.com's Customer Reviews."

> What do you most enjoy about the internet? Some people like the way the internet gives everyone a voice—anyone with internet access can express his or her opinion about anything. There are many ways people can share their opinions online: they can create their own websites and express their thoughts on social networking sites like Facebook and Twitter. In addition, people can share their thoughts by posting product reviews on websites like Amazon.com that sell these items. Amazon.com sells a wide range of objects, and the majority of items for sale on this website

have been reviewed by someone. Reviewers rate items by giving between one and five stars and can write a description of their thoughts on the item to go along with this rating. Prospective buyers should not trust these online reviews when making their purchases. Instead, consumers should rely on expert opinions and credible sources when making purchases.

This paragraph introduces its essay's claim towards the end with the text: "Prospective buyers should not trust these online reviews when making their purchases. Instead, consumers should rely on expert opinions and credible sources when making purchases." These sentences are especially important to this paragraph, as they indicate that the rest of essay will focus on the idea that consumers should not base their purchasing decisions on online reviews. Without these sentences, readers wouldn't have a clear idea of what the author intends to discuss in this essay.

To further understand how different this paragraph would be without this information, let's take a look at a revised version of it that no longer contains its final two sentences:

What do you most enjoy about the internet? Some people like the way the internet gives everyone a voice—anyone with internet access can express his or her opinion about anything. There are many ways people can share their opinions online: they can create their own websites and express their thoughts on social networking sites like Facebook and Twitter. In addition, people can share their thoughts by posting product reviews on websites like Amazon.com that sell these items. Amazon.com sells a wide range of objects, and the majority of items for sale on this website have been reviewed by someone. Reviewers rate items by giving between one and five stars and can write a description of their thoughts on the item to go along with this rating.

This revised version no longer introduces its claim; instead, it leaves readers wondering what the rest of the essay will discuss. Based on this paragraph, readers don't know for sure what the focus of the essay is or what ideas the author will continue to develop as the piece continues.

As these examples show, introducing a claim is an important component of effective argument writing. The paragraphs that introduce their pieces' claims provide a clear sense of focus that indicates the direction of the remainder of the essay. Those that don't introduce their claims provide no definite understanding of the essay's main ideas or the points to be developed in the rest of the piece. An author of a piece of argument writing who clearly and effectively states her claim is like a tour guide who communicates to her tour group exactly where the group is traveling and all of the sights they will see along the way. An author who doesn't indicate the piece's claim resembles a very different type of tour guide—one who doesn't tell the group where it is going or anything it will encounter throughout the journey. It's important that our students resemble strong tour guides in their argument writing by communicating their works' focuses and directions to their readers! In the next section, we'll take a look inside a sixth grade classroom and examine my students' work on this important tool of argument writing.

A Classroom Snapshot

Knowing that my students are big basketball fans, I begin today's lesson by connecting to their interests: "I was listening to two basketball experts on the radio," I explain, "and they were debating whether Michael Jordan or LeBron James is the best basketball player of all time. Both experts made some really good points in support of their positions and brought in some interesting evidence, but do you know what they both did at the beginning of the conversation?"

"I know!" exclaims one student, holding his hand in the air. "They introduced their claims."

"Exactly!" I reply. "Why do you think they did that?"

"Because," responds another student, "you need to introduce your claim at the beginning of an argument."

"Wonderful!" I say, praising the student's response. "You all have been doing a great job of paying attention to our conversations about introducing claims! Today, we're going to think about this aspect of argument writing in even more detail."

These students and I are in our third class discussing introducing claims in argument writing. In our first meeting, we looked at specific examples of argument writing and discussed how the authors of those pieces introduced claims in their works. In our second meeting, we discussed why introducing a claim is especially important to effective argument writing, focusing on the ways a well-focused claim provides a sense of focus to an argument essay by taking a side on an issue and establishing a foundation for the rest of the piece. To illustrate this, we examined paragraphs from argument essays with and without their claim-introducing language (as discussed in this chapter's previous section). Today, the students are going to take an even more active role in their learning: they will work in groups to analyze how opening paragraphs of argument essays would be different without the language that introduces the piece's claim. This activity builds off the previous day's discussion, but gives the students more ownership and responsibility, as each group will be responsible for identifying the claim-introducing language in the paragraph it receives, rewriting the paragraph without this language, and analyzing the differences.

I explain the activity to the class, dividing them into four separate groups and explaining that each group will receive an opening paragraph from a piece of argument writing. "Each of these paragraphs introduces a claim," I tell them. "Your job is to find the section of the paragraph that introduces the claim, rewrite the paragraph without that language, and analyze why the claim-introducing language is important to the original paragraph. I'll check in with each group while you work to see how you're doing and to talk with you about what you're noticing."

The students nod, seeming to understand the way today's activity builds off of our previous work with this concept. "Before we begin," I tell the students, "let's take a look together at an example so we can be sure we all understand what to do in this activity and how to do it. This is the first paragraph of an argumentative essay that I wrote. We'll take a look at it together and then we'll practice analyzing it." I place the opening paragraph of the argument essay, "Keep Gym Class in Schools" on the document camera, projecting the following text to the front of the room:

> The people in charge of our schools make a lot of tough decisions. Politicians, school board members, and policy makers have to think about issues like what books should be taught, whether or not schools should have dress codes, and how much time students should spend on different activities. Deciding how much time students should spend on different activities can be especially difficult. With new, challenging standards like the Common Core State Standards being used in schools and limited amounts of money, some schools have cut or reduced "specials" like gym class. These administrators should keep gym class in schools. Gym is a valuable part of the school experience that increases students' chances to live happy, successful lives and should not be eliminated.

I read the text out loud, asking the students to follow along with the projected text. Once I finish reading, I ask the students, "What is the claim of this paragraph?"

A number of student hands shoot up; I call on one who replies, "The claim is that gym class should be kept in schools."

"Very good," I respond. "Now, let's have a treasure hunt of sorts, except we're going to hunt for the claim. Where in this paragraph does the author make this claim?"

"In the last two sentences," asserts another student. "These sentences show the author's opinion about gym class being valuable. The part before that sentence talks about other things."

"Well said," I tell the student. "The first several sentences of this paragraph give background about the decisions that politicians, school board members and policy makers have to make, while the last sentences introduce the claim that gym class is important and should be kept in schools. Now, let's take a look at how this paragraph would look without these final sentences." I place the following text on the document camera, projecting it to the front of the room:

> The people in charge of our schools make a lot of tough decisions. Politicians, school board members, and policy makers have to think about issues like what books should be taught, whether or not schools should have dress codes, and how much time students should spend on different activities. Deciding how much time students should spend on different activities can be especially difficult. With new, challenging standards like the Common Core State Standards being used in schools and limited amounts of money, some schools have cut or reduced "specials" like gym class.

"Take a look at this revised version of the paragraph we just examined," I tell the students. "As you can see, it doesn't contain the sentences found in the original version that introduce the piece's claim."

"It's way different," comments a student. "This version doesn't get the same message across."

"Yeah," responds another student. "This one doesn't make any claims at all. It just gives you the background."

"Really nice responses," I say, praising the students. "So, why do you think the final sentences of the original paragraph—the ones that introduce the claim—are important?"

A number of student hands shoot into the air. I call on a young man who explains, "It's important because they tell you that the essay's going to be arguing that gym class should stay in schools. Without it, the paragraph doesn't take any sides on anything."

"That's very well put," I reply. "Without the claim-introducing language, this essay doesn't take any sides. And why is it important that this essay takes a side?"

I notice that many students have quickly raised their hands; I call on a young lady who offers, "Because it's an argument essay. It has to take a side. If we don't know what the author wants to argue, we don't really get the point of the essay."

"Excellent response," I tell the student. "You all did a great job thinking about that example. Now, it's time for you to work in your groups. As I mentioned before, I'm going to give each group an opening paragraph from a piece of argument writing. Your job is to work together to find the part of the paragraph that introduces a claim, rewrite the paragraph with that part removed, and analyze why the claim-introducing language is important to the original paragraph. While you do that, I'll check in with each group."

I divide the class into groups and give each small group an opening paragraph from an argument essay. After the groups have taken a few minutes to get started, I begin to circulate around the room and check in with different groups. I first sit down with a group that is working with the opening paragraph of an argumentative essay about the price of college.

"How are you all doing?" I ask them.

"Awesome," cheerfully replies one student in the group. "We have this paragraph here that makes the claim that college needs to cost less money."

"Very nice job identifying the claim," I respond. "Can you show me the section of the paragraph that makes this claim?"

"Sure," answers the student. She shows me the paragraph below:

> Each year, millions of young people enroll in America's colleges. Excited by the opportunities of college and optimistic about their futures, these students frequently see college as a step toward realizing their dreams. Some may dream of being teachers, others might hope to be doctors, and some might even think about being the President of the United States. College is often thought of as a time to explore new ideas by taking interesting classes, joining exciting groups, and making new friends. However, the high price of college is impacting many students' futures: the money that students need to borrow in order to attend college is limiting their opportunities after it. College needs to cost less in order to help more young people achieve their goals.

After showing me the paragraph, the student explains, "[The claim] is in the last two sentences of the paragraph."

"Great," I reply. "Now, have you all rewritten the paragraph without those two sentences?"

"We just did!" responds another student in the group. "It's right here." The student shows me a revised version of the previous paragraph, which contains the following text:

> Each year, hundreds of thousands of young people enroll in America's colleges. Excited by the opportunities of college and optimistic about their futures, these students frequently see college as a step toward realizing their dreams. Some may dream of being teachers, others might hope to be doctors, and some might even think about being the President of the United States. College is often thought of as a time to explore new ideas by taking interesting classes, joining exciting groups, and making new friends.

"Wonderful," I tell the group. "Now that you've identified the section of this paragraph that introduces the claim and you've rewritten the paragraph without the claim, I'm very excited to hear your analysis: why do you think the claim-introducing language is important to the original paragraph?"

"It's important," replies one student in the group, "because the last two sentences really show what the essay's going to be about. They show that the essay isn't just going to be about college. It's about a specific thing about college."

"Well said," I reply, "What is that specific thing?"

Another student in the group explains, "It's that college is so expensive and needs to cost less to help students do what they want in life. The last two sentences of the [original] paragraph make that point."

"Yeah," interjects another student in the group. "Those two sentences are important because of the point they make."

"Great analysis," I say. "The final two sentences of the first paragraph introduce the author's focus and show what the rest of the essay will discuss. You all did a wonderful job examining and analyzing this piece!"

I circulate around the rest of the classroom, checking in with each group and offering support and praise. Once I've spoken to each group, I address the class: "You all did a wonderful job of identifying the claim-introducing language in your paragraphs, rewriting them without that language, and analyzing the importance of that language to the original paragraph. I loved hearing your thoughts on how different these paragraphs would be without their claims—you're really getting this! Tomorrow, we'll work on creating our own pieces of argument writing and introducing the claims in them."

Recommendations for Teaching Students about Introducing Claims

In this section, I describe a step-by-step instructional process to use when teaching students about introducing claims in argument writing. The instructional steps I recommend are: 1) Show students examples of claims in argument essays, 2) Talk with students about why introducing claims is important to effective argument writing, 3) Have students analyze why claim-introducing language is important to argument writing, 4) Work with students as they introduce claims in their own pieces of argument writing, and 5) Help students reflect on why their claim-introducing statements are important to their own argument writing. Each of these recommendations is described in detail in this section.

1) Show Students Examples of Claims in Argument Essays

The first step of this instructional process is to show students examples of claim-introducing language in argument writing. By providing our students with mentor texts that illustrate what an effectively introduced claim looks like in an argumentative essay, we give them concrete models that help them understand this writing concept. I like to compare writing instruction with building a house, and the use of the mentor texts as the foundation for that construction—these examples provide a solid basis on which future instruction can build. The examples featured in this chapter are excellent models of claim-introducing language that can help your students establish strong understandings of what it means to introduce a claim in a piece of argument writing. I recommend showing students a number of examples of claim-introducing language from mentor texts so that they can see similarities and differences in the ways different argument essays introduce their claims. Once you've shown your students examples of effective claim-introducing statements, you can move to the next step of this process: thinking about why introducing claims is important to effective argument writing.

2) Talk with Students about Why Introducing Claims Is Important to Effective Argument Writing

Now that students have seen examples of how authors of argument writing introduce claims in their works, they are ready to think about why this concept is important to effective argument writing. This instructional step is rooted in this book's toolkit approach, as it focuses on why argument writers introduce their claims and what would happen if they did not do so. In order for students to understand the importance of claim-introducing language to effective argument writing, they must understand that introducing a claim enhances a piece of writing in two ways: 1) It provides a sense of focus by taking a side on an issue, and 2) It establishes a foundation for the rest of the piece.

To help students grasp the significance of introducing a claim to effective argument writing, I recommend showing them examples of introductory paragraphs from argumentative essays that introduce claims and comparing those with revised examples that no longer contain the claim-introducing language. This chapter pairs a number of paragraphs that introduce claims with revised versions that contain the same information except for the section in which the claim is introduced. For example, earlier in this chapter, we looked together at the opening paragraph of the argumentative essay "Schools Should Stay Away from Computer Grading" and explored how it differs from a revised version of that paragraph that does not include the claim-introducing language. The original paragraph indicates that the essay argues against computer programs that grade student writing, while the revised version does not provide this same sense of focus. Since it does not introduce a claim, the revised version of the paragraph does not give us a sense of what the piece argues.

3) Have Students Analyze Why Claim-introducing Language Is Important to Argument Writing

The third step of this instructional process places more responsibility on the students by asking them to analyze why introducing a claim is important to the opening paragraph of a piece of argument writing. This activity extends logically from the previous one, in which the teacher shows the students examples of paragraphs with and without claim-introducing language and talks with them about the importance of introducing a claim to effective argument writing. While the previous step was primarily teacher-directed, this one is more student-led, aligning with the gradual release of responsibility method of instruction (Pearson & Gallagher, 1983) that is central to this book. In this activity, an example of which is described in the classroom snapshot, the teacher gives students examples of paragraphs that introduce specific claims and tells the students to find the section of the paragraph that introduces the claim, rewrite the paragraph without the claim, and analyze why the claim-introducing language is important to the opening paragraph.

In the classroom snapshot, I had my students work on this activity in groups and spoke with the students in each group about their thoughts on the importance of the original claim-introducing language. This activity can also be slightly altered by having students work individually (instead of in groups) and turn in written descriptions of the claim-introducing language (instead of sharing their ideas in verbal conferences). I've conducted the activity in both formats and had success both ways—I suggest choosing the option that you feel will work best with your students. Regardless of whether the students work individually or in groups, this instructional step is a valuable one because of the ownership it places on the students and the analysis it requires them to conduct. Once you're comfortable with your students' analyses of why claim-introducing language is important to effective pieces of argument writing, you can transition them to the next step, in which they create their own claim-introducing passages.

4) Work with Students as They Introduce Claims in Their Own Pieces of Argument Writing

The fourth step of this instructional process places even more ownership on the students by asking them to create their own opening paragraphs of argument essays and to clearly introduce their claims in those paragraphs. This is an especially important step because it calls for the students to apply their knowledge of this concept to their own argumentative works. Not only does this application of knowledge help students understand the concept of introducing claims, but it also allows them to connect this writing tool to topics of interest to them. I recommend reviewing with students the many examples of argument writing they've already seen and discussed, brainstorming with them some high-interest topics they might want to discuss in their own argument writing, and then turning them loose to work on their own. While the students work, I suggest holding one-on-one conferences with them in which you check

Figure 1.1 Student Introductory Paragraph

> The whole point of using SAT scores and grades to decide who gets into a college is to make a comparison between people who want to go to the same college. The colleges want to have a system of saying that you are average, above average, or at ground zero (absolute F). However, the problem with using this system is that some people don't fit in that little box. Different ways of comparing students are needed because people don't fit in that perfect world. So, I feel that colleges should use a system that gives an extra chance for those people who don't fit in the little boxes of grades and SAT scores.

in with individual students and gauge their progress. When I confer with a student about this writing tool, I ask the student the following questions: 1) What are you arguing in this piece? and 2) Where in the piece's opening paragraph do you state this claim? I then talk with the student about whether or not the claim is clearly made and if the claim aligns with the student's goal for the piece. If there is any incongruity between these ideas, I work with the student to help him or her best align the claim in the paragraph with what he or she intends to argue.

Figure 1.1 contains an example, recently written by a student, of an introductory paragraph that introduces its claim.

The final sentence of this paragraph clearly illustrates the student's claim that colleges should think beyond grades and SAT scores when making admissions decisions.

5) Help Students Reflect on Why Their Claim-introducing Statements Are Important to Their Own Argument Writing

The final step of the instructional process is to help students reflect on why the claim-introducing statements they've written are important parts of their argumentative writings. To help students do this, I ask them to reflect on the following questions: "Why is it important that your introductory paragraph states its claim?" and "How would this paragraph be different if it didn't state its claim?" Asking students to think about these questions helps them reflect on the importance of this writing tool and see introducing one's claim as an important component of argument writing. The student who crafted the previously described introductory paragraph explained that the claim-introducing language he used is important because "It tells what side you are on and why." He explained that, "People need to know how you feel about things and you stating your claim can give them a perspective on why you think that way." He also said that, without its claim-introducing language, the paragraph "wouldn't say what I felt and why I felt that way. It would just give the facts but not why I am on that side of the topic." This student's reflections reveal his awareness of the importance of this tool to effective argument writing.

Final Thoughts on Introducing Claims

- ◆ Introducing a claim in argument writing is addressed in Common Core Writing Standards W.6.1.A, W.7.1.A, and W.8.1.A.
- ◆ An author of an argumentative essay introduces a claim by taking a position that will be further developed throughout the course of the essay.
- ◆ Introducing a claim is especially important to an effective piece of argument writing for two related reasons:
    - ◆ It provides a sense of focus by taking a side on an issue.
    - ◆ It establishes a foundation for the rest of the piece.
- ◆ When teaching students about introducing claims:
    - ◆ Show students examples of claims in argument essays.
    - ◆ Talk with students about why introducing claims is important to effective argument writing.
    - ◆ Have students analyze why claim-introducing language is important to examples of argument writing.
    - ◆ Work with students as they introduce claims in their own pieces of argument writing.
    - ◆ Help students reflect on why their claim-introducing statements are important to their own argument writing.

2

Acknowledging Alternate or Opposing Claims

What Does "Acknowledging Alternate or Opposing Claims" Mean?

An important component of a strong argumentative essay is acknowledging claims that differ from the author's argument. The Common Core Standards emphasize the importance of acknowledging alternate or opposing claims, as Standards W.7.1.A and W.8.1.A call for students to use this tactic in their argument writing. In this chapter, we'll discuss the following: what "acknowledging alternate or opposing claims" means, why this concept is important for effective argument writing, a description of a lesson on this concept, and key recommendations for helping your students acknowledge alternate or opposing claims in their own argument writing. While discussing these ideas, we'll take a look at examples of argument writing and examine alternate or opposing claims in those works.

Let's begin by considering what "acknowledging alternate or opposing claims" means. An effective argument writer does more than introduce and describe the idea she supports—she also informs her readers of other claims related to her topic that differ from the idea she supports. These claims can take a variety of forms—they can be alternative ways of thinking about a particular idea, or they can be directly oppositional to the idea for which the author is arguing. For example, the argument essay "The Importance of Baseball" addresses alternate and opposing claims to the author's contention that, despite the rise in popularity of other sports, baseball remains a significant sport. The statement, "Some detractors of baseball say that the game only remains popular and important among specific segments of the population, such as older people who enjoy a slower-paced sport or individuals in particular places where the game is disproportionately popular," provides alternative claims to the author's argument that baseball is an important sport in the 21st century. This statement doesn't directly contradict the author's claim, but does provide explanations that people who don't completely agree with the author might present by explaining that baseball is popular, but only among certain groups.

This essay also contains the following statement, which provides an opposing claim to the author's argument:

> Still others may contend that baseball's time has simply passed. These individuals may say that, while the sport was once thought of as our nation's pastime, it is no longer popular or relevant because it doesn't deliver a great deal of high-speed action like football, basketball, and automobile racing do. They may claim that we live in an age when people want high-speed, action-packed entertainment, and baseball is not relevant in a society that values these characteristics.

Here the author presents a belief that runs contrary to the essay's argument in favor of baseball's continued relevance and importance, showing that some people might argue that today's society primarily values action provided at high speeds, and baseball is not significant in today's world because many people feel the sport lacks these attributes. Table 2.1 identifies key attributes of the argumentative writing strategy of introducing alternate or opposing claims.

Now that we've examined what alternate and opposing claims are, let's move to the next section of this chapter, where we'll think about why they're important to effective argument writing.

Why Acknowledging Alternate or Opposing Claims Is Important to Effective Argument Writing

I recently worked with a seventh grade student who questioned why argument writers acknowledge alternate or opposing claims: "Why would I write about alternate or opposing claims in my essay? Isn't the essay supposed to be about *my* argument?" I told the student that this is a very good question; argument writers certainly want for their works to support their arguments, so I could see how he might find the idea of acknowledging alternate or opposing claims a bit counterintuitive. "However," I informed him, "acknowledging alternate or opposing claims is a very important part of creating an effective piece of argument writing." I explained to this student that this strategy is important to effective argument writing for two related reasons: 1) It shows that the author has considered ideas related to the piece's claim other than his or her own, and 2) It gives the author a chance to refute these ideas, which further

TABLE 2.1 Key Attributes of Introducing Alternate or Opposing Claims

Type of Claim	Description	Example
Alternate	Provides an explanation that doesn't completely contradict the author's claim, but does deliver information that might be offered by those who don't entirely agree with the author	"Some detractors of baseball say that the game only remains popular and important among specific segments of the population, such as older people who enjoy a slower-paced sport or individuals in particular places where the game is disproportionately popular."
Opposing	Presents a belief that runs contrary to the essay's argument	"Still others may contend that baseball's time has simply passed. These individuals may say that, while the sport was once thought of as our nation's pastime, it is no longer very popular or relevant, because it doesn't deliver a great deal of high-speed action like football, basketball, and automobile racing do. They may claim that we live in an age when people want high-speed, action-packed entertainment, and baseball is not relevant in a society that values these characteristics."

supports his or her claim. In this section, we'll explore each of these reasons why acknowledging alternate or opposing claims is important to effective argument writing.

Acknowledging Alternate or Opposing Claims Shows that the Author Has Considered Other Ideas

An effective piece of argument writing does more than present and describe one specific claim—it should also reveal that the author has thought carefully about other potential ideas. If an argumentative essay does not address alternate or opposing ideas, readers might not take the piece's claims as seriously. As I explained to my student who asked why argument writers should acknowledge alternate or opposing claims, "If you don't acknowledge other ideas, someone who doesn't agree with you could read your essay and say, 'The author has only thought about this from one side. He or she hasn't considered any other ideas, and therefore this argument is weak.' If you acknowledge other ideas, though, readers can't say that. Instead, you'll show that you've thought about these alternate and opposing ideas and *still* make the claim for which you're arguing. This makes your argument even stronger; leaving out these alternate and opposing claims will make your argument seem weaker."

Let's take a look at an example of an argumentative essay that acknowledges alternate and opposing claims and consider why acknowledging these claims helps strengthen the piece. In the argument essay, "Introverts Can Be Great Leaders, Too," the author presents the claim that being an outgoing extrovert is not required to be a strong leader and then acknowledges alternate and opposing claims that others may raise. The piece recognizes an opposing claim with the statement, "Some may claim that outgoing and extroverted people are best suited to leadership because extroverts can use their verbal skills to inspire others." In this passage, the author shows he has thought about the idea that extroverted leaders are preferable because of their ability to make inspirational speeches. Readers of this essay can see that the author has considered this opposing idea and has decided that, in spite of it, introverts still have the ability to be excellent leaders.

In the essay "Introverts Can Be Great Leaders, Too" the author also acknowledges an alternative claim, explaining, "Other people feel that introverts and extroverts can both be leaders in some situations, but specific situations call for extroverted leaders." By presenting this possible alternative explanation to the piece's claim, the author shows that he also considered this idea, revealing the amount of careful thought he has given to the topic. Without these opposing and alternate ideas, it may appear that the author has established the piece's claim that introverts can make excellent leaders without giving careful thought to other ways of thinking. However, by integrating these ideas, the author shows that he has considered these possible explanations while formulating his claim.

Acknowledging Alternate or Opposing Claims Gives the Author a Chance to Refute These Ideas

In addition to showing that the author has carefully considered other ideas when making a claim, acknowledging alternate or opposing ideas is important to effective argument writing because it gives the author a chance to refute these ideas. Refuting opposing ideas further supports an author's claim because it shows that the author has not only thought about the ideas the opposition might raise, but also reveals why the author believes that these ideas are not as strong as those that support his or her claim. To illustrate this, let's look at the way the essay "Introverts Can Be Great Leaders, Too" refutes the opposing and alternate claims the author introduces.

Recall the opposing claim the author of this essay acknowledges: "Some may claim that outgoing and extroverted people are best suited to leadership because extroverts can use their verbal skills to inspire others." After addressing this opposing claim, the author refutes it by stating, "However, a leader can inspire others in a variety of ways, not just through oral language. Leaders' actions and achievements can be just as inspirational as motivational speeches." This statement contributes to the effectiveness of the author's argument, as it explains why the author believes this alternate claim to be faulty. While refuting this claim, the author asserts that leaders do not need to use oral language to motivate others, and can instead do so through their actions. In this situation, acknowledging an opposing claim has provided the author with an opportunity to further argue in favor of his assertion. If this essay did not introduce this opposing claim, it would be more difficult for the reader to make this point so effectively.

Also, remember that the author of "Introverts Can Be Great Leaders, Too" acknowledges an alternative viewpoint with the statement, "Other people feel that introverts and extroverts can both be leaders in some situations, but specific situations call for extroverted leaders." The author then refutes this statement by explaining that the belief "specific situations call for extroverted leaders" is faulty, stating:

> Despite this belief that some hold, just as there are a variety of ways to inspire others, there are a variety of ways to lead in all situations. While some situations might be most commonly associated with vocal leaders, that doesn't mean introverts can't be equally successful in them. Successful sports coaches have a range of personalities and styles, from vocal to quiet, contemplative personas. Similarly, research on effective teachers shows that individuals with a wide range of personalities can become strong teachers that successfully engage and lead their students through learning activities.
>
> (Wiens & Ruday, 2014)

The author uses this statement to argue in favor of introverts' abilities to be successful leaders, problematizing common perceptions people have about leadership, drawing comparisons to varying personalities exhibited by sports coaches, and citing research that supports his argument. This is a great example of how acknowledging alternate or opposing ideas gives the author a chance to strengthen his or her argument by refuting them: providing this alternative claim gives the author of "Introverts Can Be Great Leaders, Too" a chance to show the problems with the alternative claim and introduce additional evidence that supports the essay's key argument.

So, why is addressing alternate or opposing claims important to effective argument writing? As the examples from "Introverts Can Be Great Leaders, Too" indicate, they show that an author has thought about other possible ideas and give her the opportunity to then refute those ideas. An author who has carefully considered other explanations and is able to refute them can be especially convincing, as she is able to show the reader that, despite the presence of opposing arguments, she firmly supports her piece's claim and can provide evidence that discredits these opposing statements. In the next section, we'll take a look inside a seventh grade English class and see how the students in that class work to understand the concept of acknowledging claims that differ from the author's argument.

A Classroom Snapshot

Right before class begins, one of my seventh graders rushes up to me to explain the impact that acknowledging alternate or opposing claims has had on her understanding of argument writing: "I told my older sister about how talking about the other side's claims can make your argument better. She didn't believe me at first; she was like, 'I don't get how that would make your argument better.' But then I talked to her about how acknowledging opposing claims can improve an argument for having cell phones in school. She totally got it then. I felt so smart!"

I smile, thrilled by the student's enthusiasm as well as her understanding of the importance of this concept. For the past several class periods, this student's class and I have been discussing how argument writers acknowledge alternate or opposing claims in their essays. We began by looking at examples from argument essays that acknowledge alternate or opposing claims—such as those featured in this chapter—and then discussed why acknowledging these claims is an important component of effective argument writing. Today, the students are going to take on more responsibility for their learning by working in small groups to analyze how specific examples of argument writing are enhanced when the author acknowledges alternate or opposing claims. In this activity, I will give each student group an example of an argumentative essay and ask each group to identify selections from the text that introduce alternate or opposing claims, comment on how the essay would look without those claims, and analyze how the acknowledgment of alternate or opposing claims enhances the piece.

"I love that you're thinking about acknowledging alternate or opposing claims," I tell the student, "and I love even more that you're thinking about it outside of school!"

"I used this at home, too," interjects another student who overhears our conversation. "I was telling my dad why I think the Denver Broncos will win the Super Bowl. I brought up some claims that people who disagree with me might make, and then I said why I think those claims are wrong."

"Awesome," I reply. "It's fantastic that you're thinking about this at home!" A bell rings, indicating the beginning of the period, and I address the class: "I just heard from some students who shared with me how they used the strategy of acknowledging alternate or opposing claims in conversations outside of school. I absolutely love this! You all have done such a nice job thinking about this strategy in our recent classes." I remind the students of our previous work on this topic, reviewing with them examples from argument essays that feature this strategy and recapping some reasons why this strategy is important to strong argumentative essays. After this brief review, I transition to today's activity: "Today, you're going to get to really *use* all of this knowledge you've gained about acknowledging alternate or opposing claims. I'll divide the class into groups and I'll give each group an example of an argument essay. In your groups, you'll read the essay, summarize its argument, identify the text in the essay that introduces alternate or opposing claims, and explain why you believe it is important that the author acknowledges these alternate or opposing claims. I'll give each group a guideline sheet with some key points to respond to while you do this activity." I place the guideline sheet (depicted in Figure 2.1) on the document camera and show the students that it asks them to provide the information and explanations I just mentioned to them.

After discussing the information on the guideline sheet with the students, I let them know that's it's time to move on to the activity. I divide the class of 24 students into six groups of four and give each group an argument essay to analyze as well as a guideline sheet on which to record their reactions. Once they have these materials, I begin

Figure 2.1 Group Analysis Guideline Sheet

**Group Analysis Guideline Sheet:
Acknowledging Alternate and Opposing Claims**

◆ Essay title:
◆ Summary of argument:

◆ Text that introduces alternate or opposing claims:

◆ Why you believe it is important that the author acknowledges these alternate or opposing claims:

to circulate around the classroom, checking in with groups and providing any support they need. I first check in with a group that is engaged in an intense discussion about an argumentative essay titled, "Smaller Classes, Successful Students." I sit down next to the students and compliment them on their focus: "Nice job, all of you. You all sound like you're really into this essay."

"Yeah," replies a student in the group. "It's about the importance of having small class sizes in schools."

"I really like it [the essay]," states another student. "I can really relate to it. At my last middle school, we had 38 kids in my English class! The teacher wanted to give us all one-on-one attention, but the class was way too big. Plus, there were so many papers for her to grade, so it would take a really long time for her to get them back to us."

"I love that personal connection you made," I tell the student. "It's clear that you are all thinking carefully about this topic. Now, let's think about how this piece acknowledges alternate or opposing claims. What examples did you find in this essay?"

"There's one right here," a student excitedly replies, quoting from the essay:

> There are those who believe that schools should not prioritize keeping class sizes small. Those people might say that schools are very expensive to operate and that having more students in a class allows the school to save money and avoid further cutting budgets. Schools could then use the money they save to pay for things like books, technology, sports equipment, and other items that can enhance students' school experiences. Others say that having more students in a class doesn't necessarily impact how much students learn in a particular class.

"Great job of identifying these examples," I say to the student who shared this text.

"Yeah," he replies, "this essay definitely brings up things that the opposition would say."

"Absolutely," I respond. "Now, let's think about why it's important that the author acknowledges these opposing claims. Why do you all think this is important?"

"I think it's important," shares one student, "because it [acknowledging opposing claims] shows that the author has thought about what people who disagree would say."

"Yep," interjects another student, "and this gives the author a better case. No one can say that the author hasn't thought about these other ideas—we know this author has because it's right there in the essay."

"Well said," I reply. "You're right: the author of this essay acknowledges alternate or opposing claims, which makes clear that he has considered those ideas and that he still believes he is right despite these opposing claims."

As I explain this, I am pleased to see the students nodding and clearly grasping the concept. "Now, are there any other reasons why it's important that the author acknowledges alternate or opposing claims in this essay?"

"Oh, I know!" exclaims one student. "It gives the author a chance to respond to these claims."

"That's absolutely right," I reply. "Acknowledging alternate or opposing claims gives the author a chance to reply to and refute opposing ideas. This is a really effective thing to do in argument writing. When you take an opposing claim and refute it, you actually take a potential negative and turn it into a positive for your argument."

"That's really cool," responds a student in the group. "I can totally see how that's like taking a negative and turning it into a positive."

I compliment this group on their work and continue to circulate among the different groups in the class, checking in with them and supporting their progress. Once I've spoken to each group, I address the class as a whole: "All of our groups did awesome work today. You all did really nice jobs of identifying essay sections that acknowledge alternate or opposing claims and then thinking about why it's important that the author acknowledges these alternate or opposing claims. You're doing a great job of thinking about this tool of argument writing!"

Recommendations for Teaching Students about Acknowledging Alternate or Opposing Claims

In this section, I describe a step-by-step instructional process to use when teaching students about acknowledging alternate or opposing claims in argument writing. The instructional steps I recommend are: 1) Show students examples of argument essays that acknowledge alternate or opposing claims, 2) Discuss with students why acknowledging alternate or opposing claims is an important component of effective argument writing, 3) Have students analyze why acknowledging alternate or opposing claims is important to examples of argument writing, 4) Work with students as they acknowledge alternate or opposing claims in their own argument writing, and 5) Help students reflect on why acknowledging alternate or opposing claims is important to their own argument writing. Each of these recommendations is described in detail in this section.

    1) Show Students Examples of Argument Essays that Acknowledge Alternate or Opposing Claims

I believe that showing students examples of argument essays in which the authors acknowledge alternate or opposing claims is integral to their understanding of this concept. Beginning this instructional process by showing students mentor texts in which authors acknowledge alternate or opposing claims gives students strong understandings of what this tool of argument writing can look like in practice and prepares students to think further about this concept as your instruction progresses. When I do this with my students, I place an argument essay on the classroom's document camera and read it out loud, asking students to follow along. Once I get to a place in the essay where the author has acknowledged an alternate or opposing claim, I stop and point this out to them. When recently working with a group of seventh graders, I used the essay "The Importance of Baseball" (discussed at the beginning of this chapter) to illustrate how authors acknowledge alternate or opposing claims. As the students and I examined this piece together, I identified the sections of the text where the author acknowledges alternate and opposing claims, allowing the students to see this tool of argument writing in the context of an existing essay. After we completed this activity, one seventh grader in the class acknowledged the benefits of examining mentor texts: "Seeing how the author of this baseball essay acknowledges alternate and opposing claims helped me understand what this means. It makes a lot more sense than if you just told us about this without showing us an example."

2) Discuss with Students Why Acknowledging Alternate or Opposing Claims Is an Important Component of Effective Argument Writing

Once students have seen how authors acknowledge alternate or opposing claims, they are ready to think about why this strategy is an important component of effective argument writing. When I talk with my students about the importance of this concept, I begin by explaining that acknowledging alternate or opposing claims shows that the author has considered others' ideas when reaching a conclusion. To help students understand this idea, I make specific connections to the argument essay we examined in the first recommendation. For example, I explained to my seventh graders that, by incorporating alternate and opposing claims into his essay, the author of "The Importance of Baseball" could not be accused of ignoring the opposition: "By bringing in alternate and opposing claims, the author of this essay shows readers that he's thought about this issue from the other side as well. He shows that he isn't ignoring those points of view; instead, he shows us that he's thought about them, but he still believes in his claim that baseball is important and relevant."

Next, I talk with my students about how acknowledging alternate or opposing claims allows the author to refute them. When discussing "The Importance of Baseball," I explained, "Since the author of this essay has brought in potential alternate and opposing claims, he now has a chance to further strengthen his essay by saying why those alternate or opposing claims are faulty. He can find problems in these opposing arguments, which can make his essay even stronger." When working with your students, I recommend following the same sequence I used with my seventh graders: use the examples of alternate or opposing claims you showed the students at the beginning of this process and talk with them about how acknowledging those claims helps the author show that she or he has thought about this issue from other perspectives, as well as how it gives her or him the opportunity to find faults in these alternate or opposing statements.

3) Have Students Analyze Why Acknowledging Alternate or Opposing Claims Is Important to Examples of Argument Writing

The next step of this instructional process is to give students examples of argument essays and ask them to analyze why the author's acknowledgment of alternate or opposing claims is important to the effectiveness of those essays. When doing this activity with your students, you can have them work individually or in groups to perform this analysis. This chapter's classroom snapshot describes an example of one of these activities—in that example, I divided a class of seventh graders into groups of four students, gave each group an argument essay, and asked each one to consider the following ideas: 1) The essay's argument, 2) The text in the essay that introduces alternate or opposing claims, and 3) Why the group believes it is important that the author acknowledges these alternate or opposing claims. By responding to these prompts, students can deepen their understandings of how argument authors acknowledge alternate or opposing claims in their works, as well as why acknowledging these claims is important to effective argument writing.

When conducting this activity with your students, I recommend giving each group or individual the guideline sheet depicted in Figure 2.1 to guide them as they analyze the alternate or opposing claims in the essays they're critiquing. Once the students have started working, I suggest checking with them to monitor their progress and provide support. This chapter's classroom snapshot includes a description of a conversation I had with a group of seventh graders that was working on this assignment; in this conversation, I praised the group's progress and asked probing questions to help the students in the group think in even more depth about the essay they were analyzing. Conversations like these can help us understand what our students know and what additional supports they need.

4) Work with Students as They Acknowledge Alternate or Opposing Claims in Their Own Argument Writing

Now that you've asked your students to analyze the importance of acknowledging alternate or opposing claims in argument essays, the next step is to ask them to apply this tool of effective argument writing to their own pieces. As students apply this concept to their own works, they can further enhance their understanding of it and connect it specifically to the argumentative essays they are currently writing. When I ask students to work on acknowledging alternate or opposing claims in their works, I first have them take out the pieces of argument writing they began during our discussion of introducing claims (described in Chapter 1 of this book). I then tell them to brainstorm some alternate or opposing claims that someone who feels differently about their claims might bring up. Once they've brainstormed some of these ideas, I instruct the students to pick one or two of these claims and do the following: 1) Describe why someone would make this alternate or opposing claim, and 2) Refute this claim by saying why people should agree with the point you make in your argument instead.

Figure 2.2 contains an example from a student's essay. In this essay, the student argues that more people should buy hybrid cars because of

Figure 2.2 Student Work on Acknowledging Alternate or Opposing Claims

Even though there are many great reasons why people should buy hybrid cars, there are still some people who disagree. Some people say that hybrid cars cost too much because they have a higher "sticker price" at the car dealership than normal cars do. While hybrid cars do cost more than normal ones, I want to tell people who are worried about this to look at the big picture. Drivers of hybrid cars spend far less money on gasoline than those who drive traditional cars, which means that people who buy hybrids will spend much less money on gas in the long run. A driver of a hybrid that goes 50 miles on one gallon of gasoline will purchase far less gasoline than the driver of another car that gets 30 miles on one gallon of gasoline. Also, 37 states and Washington, DC provide special rewards for people who drive hybrids or electric cars, and many of these rewards are refunds or lowered taxes (National Council of State Legislatures, 2014). This is another way that buying hybrids can save people money. Even though hybrids are often more expensive than traditional cars at first, they really help people save money over time.

the cleaner energy and better gas mileage associated with these vehicles. He acknowledges an opposing claim by stating that some may oppose hybrid cars because they generally cost more at first than traditional cars. After acknowledging this idea, the student explains his belief that this opposing claim still should not discourage potential hybrid car buyers and even identifies ways hybrid cars can help people save money.

As students work on this activity, I recommend conferencing with them individually and gauging their progress. As I conference with students, I ask them to: 1) Remind me of their pieces' claims, 2) Tell me what alternate or opposing claims they'll acknowledge in their essays, and 3) Explain how they will refute these claims. As students consider these questions, I consider their responses and ask them to further clarify and expand on the details in their responses if necessary. Once students can clearly and descriptively answer these questions, I know they are ready to discuss alternate or opposing claims in their works.

5) Help Students Reflect on Why Acknowledging Alternate or Opposing Claims Is Important to Their Own Argument Writing

I recommend concluding this instructional process by asking students to reflect on why the writing strategy of acknowledging alternate or opposing claims is important to the argument essays they're writing. This concluding step requires students to think metacognitively about this tool of effective argument writing and consider how using it in their works enhanced their pieces. When asking my seventh graders to reflect on the importance of this concept, I told them: "I want for you to understand why these writing strategies are important. Yes, I want you to use them, but I also want you to understand *why* you are using them and how they make your writing better." I suggest asking your students the following questions when asking them to reflect on the importance of acknowledging alternate or opposing claims: "Why is it important that your argument essay acknowledges alternate or opposing claims?" and "How would your essay be different if it didn't acknowledge these claims?" I like for students to first answer these questions individually in writing, then share their responses verbally with partners, and then for volunteers to share their insights with the whole class.

The student who created the paragraph on hybrid cars described in the previous recommendation commented that acknowledging alternate or opposing claims is important to his essay because "It helps me show that my claim is strong. When I bring up what others might say, like that hybrids cost too much, and then show problems with that argument, I can show that buying hybrids really is something people should do." This student explained that his essay would be different if it didn't acknowledge these claims because "If I didn't bring these things [opposing claims] up, I couldn't show that they aren't very strong. By bringing up what the opposition would say, I can show the problems with those ideas."

Final Thoughts on Acknowledging Alternate or Opposing Claims

- ◆ Acknowledging alternate or opposing claims is addressed in Common Core Writing Standards W.7.1.A and W.8.1.A.
- ◆ Effective argument writers do more than more than introduce and describe the idea they support—they also inform readers of other claims related to their topics that differ from the ideas they support.
- ◆ These claims can take two forms: alternate or opposing claims.
  - ◆ Alternate claims provide explanations that don't completely contradict the author's claim, but do deliver information that might be offered by those who don't entirely agree with the author.
  - ◆ Opposing claims present beliefs that run contrary to the essay's argument.
- ◆ Acknowledging alternate or opposing claims is important to effective argument writing for two related reasons:
  - ◆ It shows that the author has considered ideas related to the piece's claim other than his or her own.
  - ◆ It gives the author a chance to refute these ideas, which further supports his or her claim.
- ◆ When teaching students about acknowledging alternate or opposing claims:
  - ◆ Show students examples of argument essays that acknowledge alternate or opposing claims.
  - ◆ Discuss with students why acknowledging alternate or opposing claims is an important component of effective argument writing.
  - ◆ Have students analyze why acknowledging alternate or opposing claims is important to examples of argument writing.
  - ◆ Work with students as they acknowledge alternate or opposing claims in their own argument writing.
  - ◆ Help students reflect on why acknowledging alternate or opposing claims is important to their own argument writing.

3

Supporting Claims with Reasons and Evidence while Using Credible Sources

What Does It Mean to Support Claims with Reasons and Evidence while Using Credible Sources?

Strong argument writers keep two key ideas in mind when supporting their claims: 1) They use reasons and evidence to convince readers of the validity of their claims, and 2) They evaluate the credibility of the sources where they find the information used to support these claims. The Common Core State Standards emphasize the significance of these strategies: Standards W.6.1.B, W.7.1.B, and W.8.1.B call for students to support their claims with reasons and evidence and to use credible sources while doing so. In this chapter, we'll discuss the following: what it means to support claims with reasons and evidence while using credible sources, why doing so is important for strong argument writing, a description of a lesson on this concept, and key recommendations for helping your students enhance their own pieces of argument writing by supporting their claims with reasons and evidence while using credible sources. We'll examine examples of argument essays and check out how those essays support their claims with evidence drawn from credible sources.

To begin, let's think about what it means to support claims with reasons and evidence. An argument essay wouldn't be very effective if it simply introduced a claim and expected readers to believe it without any supporting reasons or evidence. Instead, argument writers need to use reasons and evidence to support any claims they make. For example, the argument essay "Schools Should Stay Away from Computer Grading" isn't written under the assumption that readers will simply believe the author's claim as soon as they read it. Instead, this essay includes reasons and evidence that support the author's argument, such as:

> A careful look at the evidence about computer grading shows that grading programs are not very reliable methods of evaluating student writing. According to a news report by Molly Bloom of NPR, Les Perelman, director of the writing center at MIT, experimented with a computer grading program and found a number of inaccuracies (Bloom, 2012). For example, when Perelman wrote a sample essay that was graded by a computer grading program, he noted that the program identified some sections of the essay as incorrect that were actually correct and didn't notice some punctuation mistakes that Perelman intentionally included. Perelman summarized the accuracy of the computer grading program by explaining, "In other words, it doesn't work very well."

This essay excerpt reveals that the author doesn't assume that readers will automatically trust the piece's claim. Instead, the author identifies a problem with computer grading and uses evidence to support the statement "grading programs are not very reliable."

Now let's take a look at the second component of this standard: the use of credible sources. Wood (2009) explains that credible sources are often current, unbiased, directed to mainstream groups, and associated with recognized and reputable organizations. In the preceding paragraph about the reliability of computer grading, the author clearly incorporates credible sources, citing a report from a mainstream, reputable news agency and integrating a quotation from a writing expert who conducted a nonbiased experiment on the topic. In the next section, we'll delve more deeply into this chapter's topics by considering why it's so important that argument writers support claims with reasons and evidence and use credible sources while doing so.

Why Supporting Claims with Reasons and Evidence while Using Credible Sources Is Important to Effective Argument Writing

The writing tool of supporting claims with reasons and evidence while using credible sources is integral to effective argument writing. Reasons and evidence grounded in credible sources enhance pieces of argument writing in two key ways. First, the use of reasons and evidence gives validity to the author's claim by supporting the essay's argument. Second, the use of credible sources assures readers that the reasons and evidence incorporated by the author are drawn from authors and news organizations that can be trusted. If an author of an argument essay did not use any reasons and evidence to support her claim and instead relied on only her own opinion, readers would not have much reason to trust the author's argument. In addition, if an author used reasons and evidence to support her claim, but relied only on biased sources, readers would probably still be skeptical. Reasons, evidence, and credible sources help an argument achieve its maximum effectiveness.

Let's take a look at how this strategy looks in practice by examining how the following excerpt from the argument essay "Keep Gym Class in Schools" supports its claim with reasons, evidence, and credible sources.

> One of the many ways gym classes benefit students is that, according to recent research, students who are physically fit perform better academically. A study published in *The Journal of Pediatrics* examined the aerobic fitness and reading and math test scores of almost 12,000 elementary and middle school students in Nebraska; the researchers found that aerobically fit students were more likely than aerobically unfit students to pass the state's reading and math tests. According to the study's authors, "to improve academic performance, schools should focus on the aerobic fitness of every student" (Rauner, Walters, Avery, & Wanser, 2013, p. 344). This study's results clearly reveal a benefit of gym classes: fit students are more likely to succeed academically.

This essay excerpt is a strong example of the importance of drawing on reasons and evidence that are rooted in credible sources to support a claim. In this paragraph, the author asserts that gym classes can have academic benefits and cites a research-based study to support this idea. The author strengthens his claim by identifying the reputable source in which the study was published, providing specific details that indicate the validity and scope of the study, and using language taken directly from the source that supports this argument. If this essay's author did not do one or more of these things, his argument would be significantly weakened. For example, if he did not incorporate specific details that illustrate the potential connection between aerobic fitness and academic performance, the author would not provide readers with any evidence in favor of the claim that gym classes can enhance academic performance. In addition, if the author did not use information from a research study published in an academic journal on pediatrics, this evidence may not have the same impact on readers. For example, if the author cited a blog or letter to an editor describing one child's experience, readers may not be as convinced as they might be when reading information about a study of nearly 12,000 children published by experts on the topic. The specific evidence and the quality of the source from which the evidence was cited help strengthen this author's argument.

As this example illustrates, supporting claims with reasons and evidence found in credible sources is important to creating an effective argument essay; without these components, an argument would not be very convincing, as it wouldn't support the validity of the author's claim. In the next section, we'll take a look inside a sixth grade classroom where I worked with students on the importance of using reasons, evidence, and credible sources to argument writing. As we'll see in this classroom snapshot, these students did an excellent job of discussing why using reasons, evidence, and credible sources is integral to strong argument writing.

A Classroom Snapshot

"I'm really excited to hear your ideas today!" I say, greeting my sixth grade class. "Today, our big question is: 'Why is supporting claims with reasons and evidence from credible sources important to good argument writing?' Why do you think we're talking about this today?"

A number of hands shoot into the air; I call on a young lady who answers, "Because we've been looking at examples of [argument] essays that have evidence that comes from credible sources."

"That's right," I reply. "In our last two classes together, we looked at examples of argument essays and discussed how the author of those essays supports his claims with reasons and evidence that were found in credible sources. Today, we're going to focus on why using reasons and evidence found in credible sources is an important tool for strong argument writing." A number of students nod, and I continue: "We're going to begin by looking at an example of argument writing that uses reasons and evidence from credible sources to support its point. Then, we'll think together about why these are important aspects of argument writing."

I put the following excerpt from the argumentative essay "Lower the Cost of College" on the document camera:

> The high costs of college are making it difficult for young college graduates to live independently. An educational research organization called The Institute for College Access and Success (TICAS) explains that two-thirds of American college graduates graduate in debt from student loans, and the average borrower will owe $26,600 in these loans (TICAS, 2013). One effect of these student loans is that more recent college graduates are living with their parents than ever before (Weissman, 2013). In an article in *The Atlantic* magazine, author Jordan Weissman explains that "61 percent more college-educated 18–34-year-olds were living with their families in 2011 than in 2001." Lauren Asher, the president of TICAS, says in an article in *Forbes* magazine that the increased student debt faced by recent graduates results in them needing to delay their independence: "Debt costs you time in savings, pushes back when and whether you can buy a home, start a family, open a small business or access capital."
>
> (Denhart, 2013)

I read the passage out loud and begin to discuss it with the students by saying, "There are three things for us to discuss about this passage. First, we'll determine the author's claim. Then, we'll talk about whether the author uses reasons and evidence to support this claim. After that, we'll determine whether the author uses credible sources for these reasons and evidence. Let's start with the first of those points: What is the claim of this passage?"

I call on a student who responds, "It's in the first sentence: 'The high costs of college make it difficult for young college graduates to live independently.'"

"Very good," I respond. "Now, do you all think this passage uses reasons and evidence to support its claim?"

Many students in the class raise their hands; I call on a student in the back of the room who shares, "Yeah, definitely."

"Can you find an example?" I ask him.

"There are a bunch of them," the student replies. "One is the part that says that two-thirds of college graduates have debt and that the average debt is $26,600."

"Excellent," I tell the student. "What other evidence is there?"

Again, a number of students raise their hands. I call on a student who explains, "There's also evidence where it says that 61 percent more college-educated 18–34-year-olds live with their families in 2011 than in 2001."

"Great," I reply. "You've done a really nice job of identifying these key pieces of evidence. Remember that I said there are three things for us to discuss about this passage in relation to our topic of the day. We've already done the first two: we've determined the author's claim and we've talked about specific pieces of evidence used to support this claim. Can someone remind us of the third topic for us to discuss related to our work today?"

I call on a student who has immediately raised her hand. "The third topic is if the evidence comes from credible sources."

"Awesome," I respond. "Remember, like we talked about last time, the word 'credible' means believable, so credible sources are those that can be easily believed or trusted. Some characteristics of credible, or believable, news sources are that they are often current, unbiased, and are connected with recognized organizations, like major newspapers, magazines, and research sources. For example, an article from a major newspaper would be considered a more credible source than a blog written by someone without any credentials on a topic. Can anyone else think of any examples of credible sources?"

"An article written by a scientist could be a credible source," answers one student.

"Good," I reply. "If you're writing about something in nature, you could use an article on the topic written by a scientist who has studied that topic. That would be a very credible source."

Another student raises a hand and explains, "If you find something in an encyclopedia, you'd have a credible source. It's unbiased and reports facts."

"Very nice," I tell the student. "I really like how you pointed out that encyclopedias are credible because they report facts in unbiased ways. Now, let's think specifically about the paragraph on college costs. Does this piece use credible sources? How can you tell?"

"I think it does," answers one student, "because the information comes from a research organization and from magazine articles."

"Yeah," interjects another student, "and the sources are pretty recent, too—they're from 2013. It's not like they're from a long time ago."

"Excellent points, both of you," I reply. "This paragraph uses information from a research organization and from national, well-respected magazines. Plus, the information here is current, which also enhances its credibility. The quotation here toward the end of the paragraph is from the president of the organization discussed in the article; this person's credentials can further enhance her credibility."

The students nod, and I move towards concluding this discussion: "You all did a really nice job today of discussing this passage. Let's close up by thinking again about our big question of the day: 'Why is supporting claims with reasons and evidence from credible sources important to good argument writing?' Based on our conversation today, why do think this is an important part of argument writing?"

Hands fly up around the room. I call on a student who states, "It's important because it can make people think what you want them to. It can convince them."

"Nicely put," I say to the student. "Why do you all think supporting claims with reasons and evidence from credible sources can convince your readers?"

"Using reasons and evidence shows the claim the author's making is based on something. It's not just something the author just came up with without any backing."

"Good," I respond. "Why is it important that these reasons and evidence come from credible sources?"

"Because," answers the same student, "that makes the evidence even more believable. If the evidence is from a source that people trust, readers will probably believe it. If it's from a source they don't trust, they probably won't believe it."

"Excellent," I reply. "You all did an excellent job today of analyzing the example I showed you and of thinking about why supporting a claim with reasons and evidence from credible sources is an important tool for effective argument writing. I'm really proud of your work and I can't wait to see even more of your work on this topic!"

Recommendations for Teaching Students about Supporting Claims with Reasons and Evidence while Using Credible Sources

In this section, I describe a step-by-step instructional process to use when teaching students how to support claims with reasons and evidence from credible sources. The instructional steps I recommend are: 1) Show students examples of argument essays that support claims with reasons and evidence from credible sources, 2) Discuss with students why supporting claims with reasons and evidence from credible sources is important to effective argument writing, 3) Ask students to analyze how much a piece of argument writing differs without reasons and evidence drawn from credible sources, 4) Support students as they use reasons, evidence, and credible sources in their own writing, and 5) Have students reflect on how supporting claims with reasons and evidence from credible sources enhances their own argument writing. Each of these recommendations is described in detail in this section.

1) Show Students Examples of Argument Essays that Support Claims with Reasons and Evidence from Credible Sources

Beginning this instructional process by showing students examples of argumentative essays that support claims with reasons and evidence drawn from credible sources ensures that students have clear understandings of what this concept looks like in practice. When recently working with the sixth grade class discussed in this chapter, I began our work on this concept by explaining that we would first examine a number of examples of argument essays that feature it: "We're going to do a whole bunch of activities related to supporting claims with reasons and evidence from credible sources, but first we're going to take a look at what this looks like. That will help all of us really understand what it means to do this." Once students have seen mentor examples of argument essays that support claims with reasons and evidence drawn from credible sources, they can think in-depth about advanced ideas related to this concept, such as why it's important to effective writing and how they can improve their own works by integrating it. I recommend doing this with your students by displaying an argument essay (such as one from this book) on a document camera and pointing out specific instances where the essay's author supports her or his point with specific pieces of evidence drawn from credible sources. As you do this, make sure students understand what the terms "reasons," "evidence," and "credible sources" mean. Once students have seen this concept on display in existing argument essays and understand the main terms associated with it, they'll be ready to move on to the next step of this process.

2) Discuss with Students Why Supporting Claims with Reasons and Evidence from Credible Sources Is Important to Effective Argument Writing

Once students have seen how the writing strategy of using reasons and evidence drawn from credible sources looks in action, you can begin talking with them about why this concept is important to effective argument writing. An example of a lesson on the importance of this writing tool is discussed in this chapter's classroom snapshot. In this snapshot, I began the lesson by posing a "Big Question": "Why is supporting claims with reasons and evidence from credible sources important to good argument writing?" The students and I worked together to answer this question by first examining an excerpt from an argument essay that supports its claims with reasons and evidence from credible sources. After reading this essay with the students, I explained to them that we would do three things with the passage: 1) Determine the author's claim, 2) Discuss whether the author uses reasons and evidence to support the claim, and 3) Decide whether the author uses credible sources for these reasons and evidence. When we finished discussing these ideas, I asked the students to return to the day's "Big Question" and reflect on why supporting claims with reasons and evidence from credible sources is important to effective argument writing.

I recommend following this sequence when helping your students understand the importance of this argument writing tool. After examining an excerpt from an argument essay with your students, work with them as they figure out what the author's claim is, whether reasons and evidence are used to support the claim, and whether the author drew from credible sources. As students discuss these topics, they are also forced to reflect on why reasons and evidence from credible sources are important to effective argument writing. For example, when students consider whether or not the sources in the essay are credible, they must consider why these sources are or are not credible and how the quality of the source ultimately affects the impact of the passage. Once you and the students have discussed each of these issues, the students should be well-prepared to answer the day's "Big Question." If the students can thoughtfully answer this question, you can be confident that they understand the significance of this concept and are ready to move to the next step of this instructional process.

3) Ask Students to Analyze How Much a Piece of Argument Writing Differs without Reasons and Evidence Drawn from Credible Sources

This step of the instructional process builds off of the previous stages: since students have now seen examples of reasons and evidence drawn from credible sources and talked with you about why the use of this information is important to effective argument writing, they're ready to take on even more responsibility. I recommend giving students this increased responsibility by asking them to work individually or in small groups to analyze how much a piece of argument writing would differ without reasons and evidence drawn from credible sources. This activity gives the students a chance to think in even more depth about why reasons, evidence, and credible sources are important to argument essays and allows them to take on more ownership of the activity than the previous step in this instructional process, which is primarily teacher-led.

I recently did this activity with my sixth graders by dividing them into small groups, giving each group an example of an argument essay to analyze, and asking each group to do the following: 1) Find a section of the essay that uses reasons and evidence drawn from credible sources, 2) Rewrite that section without reasons and evidence that come from credible sources, and 3) Share these two passages with the class and explain why the reasons and evidence drawn from credible sources are important to the effectiveness of the essay. One group of students in my class completed this activity using an argument essay titled "Don't Trust Amazon.com's Customer Reviews." First, they identified the following section of the essay as an example of an author using reasons and evidence drawn from credible sources:

Online reviews may be written by very biased sources. A 2013 *New York Times* article described an investigation by New York law-enforcement agents of companies that create fake online reviews and businesses that hire these companies to do so (Streitfeld, 2013). This article, titled "Giving yourself 5 stars? Online, it might cost you," explains that some businesses have been paying so-called "reputation" companies to write positive online reviews of their products—regardless of whether or not these reviews are accurate. The article quotes Eric Schneidermann, the New York Attorney General, who argues that fake online reviews are especially dishonest: "When you look at a billboard, you can tell it's a paid advertisement—but on Yelp or Citysearch, you assume you're reading authentic consumer opinions, making this practice even more deceiving." Fake online reviews have become so problematic and widespread that researchers from Cornell University have developed a computer program designed to detect dishonest reviews (Ott, Choi, Cardie, & Hancock, 2011). The combination of the New York investigation and the need for the Cornell computer program strongly suggests that online reviews have the strong possibility of being untrustworthy.

Next the students reworked this paragraph so it no longer contained reasons and evidence drawn from credible sources. Instead of citing reputable news sources, quoting experts, and discussing research from a major university as the original text does, the reworked version contained statements like "My brother says you can't believe online reviews" and "I don't trust online reviews because I don't think people are usually honest." As one of the students in this group explained to me, "The original essay uses real evidence from trustworthy sources. When we redid it, we used people's opinions that weren't based on any evidence and definitely weren't from trustworthy sources." Another member of the group described why the reasons and evidence drawn from credible sources were important to the original essay: "They're important because they show that experts believe this is a problem. Readers will be more convinced that something's a problem if there's evidence from experts that shows it. They won't be convinced if it's just my opinion with nothing to support it."

4) Support Students as They Use Reasons, Evidence, and Credible Sources in Their Own Writing

This step releases even more responsibility to the students by asking them to apply the argument writing tool of using reasons and evidence drawn from credible sources to their own works. I suggest opening this activity by reminding the students of the characteristics of credible sources so that they're well-positioned to find their own while they write. In addition, I recommend giving students access to a laptop cart, computer lab, or library so that they have access to a number of sources from which they can draw as they work. Once you feel the students are ready to get started, allow them to work independently on their own pieces of argument writing and check in with them about the reasons, evidence, and credible sources they're using to support the points in their works.

When recently working on this activity with my sixth graders, I spoke with a student who was writing an essay that argued that young baseball players should limit the amount of pitches they throw in order to prevent arm injuries as they get older. As I conferred with him, I learned that he worked hard to find articles from credible sources that support his point: "I've got a bunch of research articles that say that kids who pitch shouldn't pitch nearly as much as they do," explained the student. "I found one that says that too many kids play baseball year-round, and that pitching too much when you're young leads to elbow and shoulder injuries when you get older. That's why, according to these articles, so many major league pitchers have elbow and shoulder problems." This student continued to explain that these research articles were published in reputable sources and were written by experts in the field: "These [articles] are all published in respectable places, like national sources, and are based on facts. One was written by James Andrews, who is talked about on ESPN all the time because all the pro athletes go to him for their operations." This student's comments show his awareness of the attributes of credible sources and suggest his understanding of the importance of using evidence from them. As this student continued to research this topic, he grew even more invested in it, eventually creating a blog on sports-related safety for young athletes where he posted this essay and other related thoughts. "I always make sure I use evidence that comes from credible sources when I write on the blog," he later told me.

5) Have Students Reflect on How Supporting Claims with Reasons and Evidence from Credible Sources Enhances Their Own Argument Writing

I recommend concluding this instructional process by asking students to reflect on the importance of this concept to effective argument writing. I like to do this by asking students the following question: "How would your piece of argument writing be different if it didn't support its claims with reasons and evidence drawn from credible sources?" This question requires students to consider why supporting claims with reasons and evidence from credible sources is an important tool that has enhanced their own argumentative essays, increasing their metacognitive awareness of the significance of this concept. The student who wrote about preventing baseball players' arm injuries responded to this question by saying, "My essay would be totally different without the evidence it has. I used really credible sources, like research done by experts like Dr. James Andrews. That makes people a lot more likely to believe what I'm writing, so it definitely makes my argument stronger."

Final Thoughts on Supporting Claims with Reasons and Evidence while Using Credible Sources

- ◆ Supporting claims with reasons and evidence while using credible sources is addressed in Common Core Writing Standards W.6.1.B, W.7.1.B, and W.8.1.B.
- ◆ Credible sources are often current, unbiased, directed to mainstream groups, and associated with recognized and reputable organizations (Wood, 2009).
- ◆ Reasons and evidence grounded in credible sources enhance pieces of argument writing in two key ways:
  - ◆ First, the use of reasons and evidence gives validity to the author's claim by supporting the essay's argument.
  - ◆ Second, the use of credible sources assures readers that the reasons and evidence incorporated by the author are drawn from authors and news organizations that can be trusted.

- ◆ When teaching students about supporting claims with reasons and evidence while using credible sources:
  - ◆ Show students examples of argument essays that support claims with reasons and evidence from credible sources.
  - ◆ Discuss with students why supporting claims with reasons and evidence from credible sources is important to effective argument writing.
  - ◆ Ask students to analyze how much a piece of argument writing differs without reasons and evidence drawn from credible sources.
  - ◆ Support students as they use reasons, evidence, and credible sources in their own writing.
  - ◆ Have students reflect on how supporting claims with reasons and evidence from credible sources enhances their own argument writing.

4

Organizing Reasons and Evidence Logically

What Does "Organizing Reasons and Evidence Logically" Mean?

Another key component of argument writing is logically organizing the reasons and evidence used to support an author's point. This argument writing tool extends from the one discussed in the preceding chapter— supporting claims with reasons and evidence drawn from credible sources. Once argument writers have found reasons and evidence drawn from credible sources to support their points, they need to organize them logically so they make sense to the reader and support the essay's claim as effectively as possible. The Common Core State Standards address the significance of this writing strategy, as Standards W.6.1.A, W.7.1.A, and W.8.1.A identify its importance. In this chapter, we'll explore the following: what "organizing reasons and evidence logically" means, why it is important for effective argument writing, a description of a lesson on this concept, and key recommendations for helping middle school writers organize reasons and evidence logically in their own argument essays. As we do this, we'll look at examples of argument writing and examine how those pieces organize reasons and evidence logically.

Let's begin by discussing what "organizing reasons and evidence logically" means. An effective argument writer doesn't simply list unorganized pieces of evidence that support a particular claim. Instead, a successful author uses paragraphs to group related information together and provide readers with an organized, easy-to-comprehend piece. In addition, a strong argument writer will sequence these paragraphs in a clear, logical way. Ramage, Bean, and Johnson (2010) describe a "Classically Structured" argument essay as having the following components: 1) An introduction (which contains the author's claim), 2) A description of the author's position, 3) A summary of opposing views, 4) A response to these opposing views, and 5) A conclusion. If our students' argument essays contain these components and group related information together, their own works will contain logically organized reasons and evidence.

To further illustrate this concept, let's explore what it can look like in action. The argument essay "The Importance of Baseball" groups related pieces of information together and presents them in a way that logically supports the author's claim that baseball is still relevant and important in the 21st century. After presenting readers with an introduction that states the piece's claim, the author proceeds to develop his position, using the following paragraph that discusses baseball's global significance:

> One indicator of baseball's importance is its global popularity. Although it has been traditionally called America's "National Pastime," baseball has been embraced by athletes in countries around the world. One example of this is the World Baseball Classic, a tournament in which countries from all over the globe compete. The World Baseball Classic has grown so much in popularity around the world that event organizers increased the amount of competing countries from 16 in 2009 to 28 in 2013 (MLB, 2011). In addition, games of the 2013 World Baseball Classic were played in four different countries: Japan, Puerto Rico, Taiwan, and the United States of America (Sports Illustrated for Kids, 2013). The World Baseball Classic is a key representation of baseball's global appeal.

The author of this piece then continues the essay by presenting readers with other paragraphs that support the essay's claim in additional ways (such as the significance of baseball to American history), claims made by detractors, rebuttals to those claims, and a concluding section. In the next section, we'll explore this topic even further by delving into why organizing reasons and evidence logically is especially important to effective argument writing.

Why Organizing Reasons and Evidence Logically Is Important to Effective Argument Writing

I recently spoke with a middle school English teacher named Rebecca whose classroom experience reveals the importance of organizing reasons and evidence logically when writing arguments: "My students are good at finding evidence [to support their claims], but they're having a hard time organizing that evidence when they write. Even when they use paragraphs, they still struggle with making sure all the information in each paragraph is related. It really makes their essays hard to follow." Rebecca's comment sheds light on why organizing reasons and evidence logically is important to effective argument writing: this writing strategy creates a structure that is easy to understand and effectively supports the author's claim. Without logically organized reasons and evidence, a reader may get distracted by the piece's lack of structure and not fully comprehend the information used to support the author's claim.

Let's further consider the importance of this concept by taking a look at two paragraphs from the argument essay "Smaller Classes, Successful Students." Each of these paragraphs supports the author's claim that small class sizes can enhance students' chances to be successful in school.

> Research suggests that teaching students in small classes can maximize students' chances of being successful later in life. For example, a study published in Columbia University's *Teachers College Record* in 2001 called "The Enduring Effects of Small Classes" states that students who are in small classes in early grades are more likely than students in larger classes to get higher grades, score better on standardized tests, graduate from high school, and go to college (Finn, Gerber, Achilles, & Boyd-Zaharias, 2001). The findings of this study make a compelling case for keeping class sizes small, as the increased chances of these long-term successes are important for not only our students but society as a whole.
>
> In addition, smaller class sizes can reduce the number of teachers leaving their profession. The National Commission on Teaching and America's Future reported in 2007 that close to 50 percent of new teachers leave teaching within five years, and a 2002 New York City Department of Education report stated that excessive class size was a major reason teachers left their jobs after only one year (Gallagher, 2002). If schools can maintain smaller class sizes, they can eliminate this significant reason for teachers leaving their jobs, providing schools with continuity and reducing the constant need for schools to train and develop novice teachers.

The author of these paragraphs has organized the reasons and evidence in them logically: each paragraph contains related information that supports the paragraph's key idea. The evidence in the first paragraph develops the statement that small classes can enhance students' chances of living successful lives, while the evidence in the second paragraph focuses on how small classes can reduce the high level of teacher turnover that currently exists. To further illustrate the importance of organizing reasons and evidence logically, let's take a look at what these paragraphs would look like if they were not divided into separate paragraphs and were instead grouped together into a large chunk of text:

> Research suggests that teaching students in small classes can maximize students' chances of being successful later in life. For example, a study published in Columbia University's *Teachers College Record*

in 2001 called "The Enduring Effects of Small Classes" states that students who are in small classes in early grades are more likely than students in larger classes to get higher grades, score better on standardized tests, graduate from high school, and go to college. The findings of this study make a compelling case for keeping class sizes small, as the increased chances of these long-term successes are important for not only our students but society as a whole. In addition, smaller class sizes can reduce the number of teachers leaving their profession. The National Commission on Teaching and America's Future reported in 2007 that close to 50 percent of new teachers leave teaching within five years, and a 2002 New York City Department of Education report stated that excessive class size was a major reason teachers left their jobs after only one year. If schools can maintain smaller class sizes, they can eliminate this significant reason for teachers leaving their jobs, providing schools with continuity and reducing the constant need for schools to train and develop novice teachers.

This text does not have the same sense of organization as the original text; all of the information is combined in one very large paragraph, which impacts the reader's experience in making sense of it. When the information is divided into separate paragraphs and each paragraph focuses on supporting a specific idea related to the essay's claim, readers can use the piece's organization to help them understand the text and identify supporting reasons and evidence. The distinctions between the original text and the new version that clumps all of this information together illustrates the importance of organizing reasons and evidence: an organized piece reveals its key ideas and supporting details much more clearly than one that does not. In the next section, we'll take a look inside a seventh grade classroom and examine how the students in this class analyze the importance of organizing reasons and evidence logically.

A Classroom Snapshot

"Are you all ready for a challenge?" I say as I enthusiastically begin class with my seventh graders. "Because I have one for you today!"

"What is it?" asks a young lady sitting in the front of the room.

"Today," I reply, "you all are going to practice organizing reasons and evidence logically in argument writing. In today's class, we're going to get into groups and I'm going to give each group a large chunk of text from an argument essay that should be organized better and divided into separate paragraphs. Your group's job will be to do the following: 1) Decide where the text should be divided into separate paragraphs, 2) Explain why it should be divided there, and 3) Discuss why dividing the text into separate paragraphs enhances the piece."

This is our third class focusing on the argument writing tool of organizing reasons and evidence logically. In our first meeting, I showed the students examples of argument essays and pointed out the ways the author of those essays organizes evidence logically by dividing separate ideas into distinct paragraphs. In our next class, the students and I discussed why organizing reasons and evidence logically is important to strong argument writing, focusing on how a well-organized piece is easy for readers to understand and clearly supports the author's claim. While discussing these ideas, we examined an excerpt from an argument essay and then considered how that essay would look if it did not use paragraphs to organize its reasons and evidence into separate sections. Today's activity builds off of our last discussion, but gives the students more ownership and responsibility.

I divide the students into small groups and give each group a paper containing a large piece of text adapted from an argument essay, which they are responsible for dividing into separate paragraphs and analyzing. I also give each group the guideline sheet depicted in Figure 4.1, explaining that each group will record key points of its analysis on this sheet.

Figure 4.1 Group Guideline Sheet

Group Guideline Sheet: Organizing Reasons and Evidence
◆ Between which sentences did you divide your passage into separate paragraphs?
◆ Why did you divide it there?
◆ Why does dividing the passage into separate paragraphs enhance it?

"As you work," I tell the students, "I'm going to circulate around the room and check in with each group. I'm going to ask you to talk to me about the points on your guideline sheet: where you divided the text, why you divided it there, and how dividing it there enhances the passage."

I give the students a few minutes to get started and then begin circulating and talking with the groups. I sit down with a group that is working with the following passage from the argument essay "Introverts Can Be Great Leaders, Too":

> Many effective leaders throughout history have been introverts. Jennifer Kahnweiler, in her 2009 book *The Introverted Leader*, identifies famous executives and leaders such as Bill Gates, Mother Theresa, and Abraham Lincoln as naturally introverted. In many ways, explains Kahnweiler, these leaders may have actually been helped by being introverted, as introverts are especially good at thinking and processing their ideas before acting. The introverted nature of these people shows that introverts have held leadership roles for a long time and suggests that they will continue to do so in the future. Not only can introverts and extroverts both be effective leaders, but research published in 2010 in the *Harvard Business Review* explains that, when employees of a company are proactive and offer ideas to improve the company, introverted leaders are more effective than extroverted ones (Grant, Gino, & Hofman, 2010). The introverted leaders described in the study "listened carefully and made employees feel valued, motivating them to work hard." The authors of this study explain that "it's worth reexamining that stereotype" that effective leaders are always extroverts, as there are many situations where this is not the case.

"Hey everyone," I say, greeting the group. "Tell me what you're noticing about this passage."

"It should be two separate paragraphs, so we divided it into two paragraphs right here," explains one student, indicating that he means between the sentence, "The introverted nature of these people shows that introverts have held leadership roles for a long time and suggests that they will continue to do so in the future" and the following one, which reads, "Not only can introverts and extroverts both be effective leaders, but research published in 2010 in the *Harvard Business Review* explains that, when employees of a company are proactive and offer ideas to improve the company, introverted leaders are more effective than extroverted ones (Grant, Gino, & Hofman, 2010)."

"Good," I reply. "Now, talk to me about why you divided it there."

"It's where the author goes from talking about one idea to talking about another," replies another student in the group. "The author starts off talking about historical people who are introverts and leaders, and then, starting with the sentence where we'd make a new paragraph, goes into talking about research from the *Harvard Business Review*."

"Wonderful!" I exclaim. "I really like the way you mention how the author shifts from one idea to another at this point in the passage, and that you'd use that shift to make a new paragraph. Let's think now about the next question on your guideline sheet: 'Why does dividing the passage into separate paragraphs enhance it?' What do you all think?"

"It definitely makes the passage more organized," states a student.

"Good," I reply. "Why do you feel that it does?"

"Because," explains the student, "it makes it so that the passage is divided into different topics. Without dividing it into paragraphs, it's just a big thing of words. When it's divided into two paragraphs and those paragraphs are about separate topics, the passage is a lot easier to understand."

"Plus," interjects another student in the group, "if it was divided where we said it should be, the reasons and evidence would be more organized and not just in one big chunk."

"Excellent job," I tell the students. "Those explanations showed a good understanding of how dividing this passage into related paragraphs organizes the reasons and evidence here clearly and logically, which definitely makes the passage easier to understand. Great work! You might also be interested to know that the real version of this argument essay is divided into paragraphs in the same place you identified, so you're thinking right along with the author. Fantastic, you all."

The students in this group smile and I continue to circulate around the room, checking in with the rest of the groups and talking with them about their responses to the questions on the guideline sheet. I'm very pleased to see that each group has done an excellent job of dividing their passage into separate paragraphs when the author of the piece moves from one idea to the other. In addition, each group shows an excellent understanding of why dividing the piece at that point can enhance the passage. I close the day's session by addressing the class: "Wonderful job today, you all. I'm so happy with how carefully you thought about where to divide your group's passage and how dividing it in that way can enhance your passage by organizing the reasons and evidence the author presents. Next time, we're going to focus on logically organizing the reasons and evidence in our own writing! I can't wait to see what you do—I'm sure it will be awesome!"

Recommendations for Teaching Students about Organizing Reasons and Evidence Logically

In this section, I describe a step-by-step instructional process to use when teaching students how to organize reasons and evidence logically. The instructional steps I recommend are: 1) Show students examples of argument essays that organize reasons and evidence logically, 2) Talk with students about why organizing reasons and evidence logically is important to effective argument writing, 3) Ask students to analyze the significance of logically organized reasons and evidence, 4) Confer with students as they organize reasons and evidence in their own argument writing, and 5) Ask students to reflect on how logically organizing reasons and evidence enhances their own argument essays. Each of these recommendations is described in detail in this section.

1) Show Students Examples of Argument Essays that Organize Reasons and Evidence Logically

Beginning this process by showing students examples of argument essays that organize reasons and evidence logically allows them to see this concept in practice, ensuring a clear understanding of what it means. The middle school teacher named Rebecca referred to earlier in this chapter explained that showing examples of logically organized reasons and evidence to her students was instrumental in helping them understand the concept: "I think showing my students examples of essays [that logically organize reasons and evidence] was the turning point for them in terms of helping them understand it. It was like things started to click for them once they saw these examples." Research on mentor text use supports Rebecca's comment; showing students examples of effective writing helps them learn a wide range of skills, including tactics related to organization and structure (Ehmann & Gayer, 2009). When you show your students examples of argument essays that use this tool effectively, you build their knowledge of what it means to logically organize reasons and evidence. Once students have developed this background knowledge, they can progress to the next step of this instructional process.

2) Talk with Students about Why Organizing Reasons and Evidence Logically Is Important to Effective Argument Writing

After you've shown students what it means to logically organize reasons and evidence in argument writing, I recommend talking with them about why this writing tool is an important part of creating effective argument essays. When I have these conversations with my students, I help them understand that a clearly and logically organized piece is much easier to comprehend—and therefore much more convincing—than one that does not organize its reasons and evidence well. If reasons and evidence aren't well-organized, I tell my students, readers might not understand the information in the essay and won't be swayed by the piece's argument.

I suggest facilitating these conversations by showing students examples of effective argument essays that organize their reasons and evidence into paragraphs and then presenting students with the same information no longer grouped into separate paragraphs. For example, earlier in this chapter, I described the importance of this concept by displaying two clearly organized paragraphs from the argument essay "Smaller Classes, Successful Students" and then comparing them with a new version, which combined all of the information in these two paragraphs into one long paragraph. While the first version of this excerpt organized different types of information into distinct paragraphs, the second grouped it all together, making it harder to understand the evidence. After conducting a similar activity with my seventh graders, a student did an excellent job of summarizing the importance of this concept: "This really makes sense," the student explained. "[If] you spend all this time writing an argument essay, you don't want for a lousy structure to make it so people can't understand it. You want to organize it real well so people will understand all the evidence you're giving." By talking with your students about the significance of this writing tool and showing them examples that illustrate its value, they too can grasp why it's important to effective argument writing!

3) Ask Students to Analyze the Significance of Logically Organized Reasons and Evidence

The third step of this instructional process is related to the previous discussion of the importance of logically organizing reasons and evidence, but differs because of the increased responsibility it gives students. Instead of just discussing the significance of the concept, this step uses an activity that requires students to put the concept into action and then reflect on it. This activity, an example of which is discussed in this chapter's classroom snapshot, begins with giving students an excessively long passage that should be divided into separate paragraphs. (To create one of these passages, just take two or three paragraphs from one of the argument essays in Appendix A and combine them into one long paragraph.) Once I've given students these passages, I ask them to decide where the text should be divided into paragraphs, explain why it should be divided there, and discuss why dividing the passage into paragraphs improves it.

I've found this activity to be especially useful because of the way it combines hands-on practice with students' analysis. The three tasks students complete in this activity require them to gradually use more complex higher-order thinking skills. The group described in the classroom snapshot provides a good example of this: they began with identifying where to divide their passage into separate paragraphs and concluded with an insightful comment on how dividing a large chunk of text into clearly organized groups of information makes it easier to understand. Once this group completed its analysis, I was confident in its members' awareness of how to put this writing tool into action and why it is important. Given the students' strong performance on this activity, I knew they were ready for the next step: putting this concept into practice in their own argument writing.

4) Confer with Students as They Organize Reasons and Evidence in Their Own Argument Writing

At this point in the instructional process, the students are ready to take even more ownership over their work by applying this concept to their own argument writing. I recommend asking students to put this writing strategy into action in two ways: first, by examining any argument writing they've already done and evaluating whether or not they've used paragraphs to logically organize the reasons and evidence they've included, and then by using this strategy as they continue to compose these essays. While my students work on these activities, I move around the room and confer with each of them individually, talking with them about the logical organization of reasons and evidence in their works.

I recently conferred with a middle schooler who was working on an argument essay asserting that standardized tests should be de-emphasized in today's schools. When I asked him how he had applied the strategy of logically organizing reasons and evidence to this piece, he replied, "I looked back at what I've already written and found a place where I can organize the information better. Right here, I talk about how standardized tests take away teaching time and in the same paragraph I talk about how they put too much pressure on students. I think it would be better and more organized if I made these into separate paragraphs." The student's comments show a specific way he applied this argument writing tool to his work; by dividing the information he describes into separate paragraphs, he enhanced the logical organization of reasons and ideas in his piece.

5) Ask Students to Reflect on How Logically Organizing Reasons and Evidence Enhances Their Own Argument Essays

I recommend concluding this instructional process by having students reflect on how the logical organization of reasons and evidence benefits their own works, as this helps them further consider the importance of this strategy to effective argument writing. When doing this, I suggest writing the following questions on the board and then asking students to reflect on them: "How would your essay be different if you didn't logically organize the reasons and evidence in it?" and "Based on this, why do you think logically organizing reasons and evidence is important to good argument writing?" I like to have students think about these questions individually, tell their ideas to a partner, and then volunteer to share their responses with the rest of the class.

The student discussed in the preceding recommendation who wrote about standardized tests reflected on the importance of logically organizing the reasons and evidence in his piece by saying, "My essay would be way different if I didn't logically organize the reasons and evidence in it. Right now, it has a good order, with an introduction, different paragraphs that talk about evidence that supports my point, and then a conclusion. If it didn't have this order and didn't divide information into separate paragraphs, it would be much harder to understand. Organizing reasons and evidence logically definitely is important to argument writing because your writing makes a lot more sense if you do it." This response reveals the student's understanding of the impact this argument writing tool has on his work and how much his essay would differ without logically organized reasons and evidence.

Final Thoughts on Organizing Reasons and Evidence Logically

- ◆ Organizing reasons and evidence logically is addressed in Common Core Writing Standards W.6.1.A, W.7.1.A, and W.8.1.A.
- ◆ A successful author logically organizes reasons and evidence by using paragraphs to group related information together and sequencing these paragraphs in a clear, logical way.
- ◆ Organizing reasons and evidence logically is important to effective argument writing because a clearly and logically organized piece is much easier to comprehend—and therefore much more convincing—than one that does not organize its reasons and evidence well.
- ◆ When teaching students about organizing reasons and evidence logically:
  - ◆ Show students examples of argument essays that organize reasons and evidence logically.
  - ◆ Talk with students about why organizing reasons and evidence logically is important to effective argument writing.
  - ◆ Ask students to analyze the significance of logically organized reasons and evidence.
  - ◆ Confer with students as they organize reasons and evidence in their own argument writing.
  - ◆ Ask students to reflect on how logically organizing reasons and evidence enhances their own argument essays.

5

Using Words, Phrases, and Clauses to Create Cohesion and Clarify Relationships

What Does "Using Words, Phrases, and Clauses to Create Cohesion and Clarify Relationships" Mean?

Another important tool for creating well-organized argument essays that are easy to understand is the strategy of using words, phrases, and clauses to create cohesion and clarify relationships when presenting readers with claims, counterclaims, reasons, and evidence. The Common Core State Standards address the importance of this concept: Standards W.6.1.C, W.7.1.C, and W.8.1.C call for students to use this strategy in their argument writing. In this chapter, we'll discuss the following: what "using words, phrases, and clauses to create cohesion and clarify relationships" means, why this concept is important for effective argument writing, a description of a lesson on this concept, and key recommendations for helping your students effectively apply this concept to their own argument writing. We'll also examine a number of examples of argument essays that utilize this tool and explore how those works create cohesion and clarify relationships.

First, let's discuss what it means to use words, phrases, and clauses to create cohesion and clarify relationships. In order to make their essays as clear as possible, authors of argument essays use certain words, phrases, and clauses to connect the ideas in their works and show the ways these ideas relate to one another. For example, if an author is connecting similar ideas, she might use language like "for example," "in addition," "another," and "because," as all of these examples can link related points. If an author wants to show that two ideas are dissimilar in some way, she might use "however," "in contrast," or "despite this" to call the reader's attention to these differences. Whether authors are highlighting similarities or differences in the information they present, they are still applying this tool of argument writing by clarifying the relationships between the ideas in their works.

Let's take a look at an example of an argument essay that utilizes this strategy. The following excerpt from the argument essay "Schools Should Stay Away from Computer Grading" uses the phrase "for example" to connect two related statements and to show that the information in the second sentence is an example of the first:

> According to a news report by Molly Bloom of NPR, Les Perelman, director of the writing center at MIT, experimented with a computer grading program and found a number of inaccuracies (Bloom, 2012). For example, when Perelman wrote a sample essay that was graded by a computer grading program, he noted that the program identified some sections of the essay as incorrect that were actually correct and didn't notice some punctuation mistakes that Perelman intentionally included.

Another argument essay that implements this argument writing tool is "Lower the Cost of College," which uses the word "however" to indicate the differences between two statements. This excerpt first explains the positive attributes of college, but then shifts to a description of how college costs are negatively impacting college students; the author uses "however" to signal this shift:

> College is often thought of as a time to explore new ideas by taking interesting classes, joining exciting groups, and making new friends. However, the high price of college is impacting many students' futures: the money that students need to borrow in order to attend college is limiting their opportunities after it.

As these examples illustrate, words, phrases, and clauses that create cohesion and clarify relationships are frequently used in argument essays. In the next section, we'll explore in detail why this strategy is especially important to strong argument writing.

Why Using Words, Phrases, and Clauses to Create Cohesion and Clarify Relationships Is Important to Effective Argument Writing

The writing strategy of using words, phrases, and clauses to create cohesion and clarify relationships is important because it clearly communicates to readers how statements and ideas relate to one another. By doing so, this writing tool makes a piece much easier to comprehend than if the author did not carefully select words, phrases, and clauses to establish these relationships. Let's begin exploring the significance of this concept by critiquing an example from the argument essay "The Importance of Baseball." In the following example, the author uses the phrase "in addition" to express the relationship between the ideas in two sentences:

> The World Baseball Classic has grown so much in popularity around the world that event organizers increased the amount of competing countries from 16 in 2009 to 28 in 2013 (MLB, 2011). In addition, games of the 2013 World Baseball Classic were played in four different countries: Japan, Puerto Rico, Taiwan, and the United States of America.
>
> (Sports Illustrated for Kids, 2013)

The author's use of "in addition" is especially important to the cohesion of this passage, as it indicates that the information in both of these statements supports the idea that the World Baseball Classic is increasing in global popularity. Without this phrase, the passage would read as follows:

> The World Baseball Classic has grown so much in popularity around the world that event organizers increased the amount of competing countries from 16 in 2009 to 28 in 2013 (MLB, 2011). Games of the 2013 World Baseball Classic were played in four different countries: Japan, Puerto Rico, Taiwan, and the United States of America.
>
> (Sports Illustrated for Kids, 2013)

In this revised example—with "in addition" omitted—the text has a different feel; it doesn't directly indicate the relationship between the information in these sentences. The original passage clearly links each of these statements, but the new passage does not provide the same cohesion. The phrase "in addition" is important to this essay because, when this phrase is removed, this passage does not convey the same linkage between ideas that the original text does. Table 5.1 compares these two excerpts and highlights the differences between them. A reproducible template of this chart is included in Appendix B.

Now, let's take a look at another example of how an argument writer creates cohesion and clarifies relationships. In the following excerpt from "Don't Trust Amazon.com's Customer Reviews," the author uses the phrase "despite these widespread beliefs" to indicate that two sentences contain contrasting ideas:

> People who hold this belief might feel that it is useful to read comments from anyone who wants to review an item, regardless of that person's qualifications. Despite these widespread beliefs,

TABLE 5.1 Text Comparison from "The Importance of Baseball" Excerpt

Original Text	Text with Word, Phrase, or Clause that Creates Cohesion and Clarifies Relationships Removed	Why the Word, Phrase, or Clause that Creates Cohesion and Clarifies Relationships Is Important
The World Baseball Classic has grown so much in popularity around the world that event organizers increased the amount of competing countries from 16 in 2009 to 28 in 2013 (MLB, 2011). In addition, games of the 2013 World Baseball Classic were played in four different countries: Japan, Puerto Rico, Taiwan, and the United States of America (Sports Illustrated for Kids, 2013).	The World Baseball Classic has grown so much in popularity around the world that event organizers increased the amount of competing countries from 16 in 2009 to 28 in 2013 (MLB, 2011). Games of the 2013 World Baseball Classic were played in four different countries: Japan, Puerto Rico, Taiwan, and the United States of America (Sports Illustrated for Kids, 2013).	The phrase "in addition" is important to the original passage because it indicates that the information in both of these statements supports the idea that the World Baseball Classic is increasing in global popularity. Without this phrase, this passage does not link its ideas as effectively as the original text does.

this availability to the general public is precisely the problem with online reviews; when all people can review items, there is no guarantee that the reviewers will be knowledgeable about a product and present an unbiased opinion.

This phrase is important to this passage because of the way it communicates to the reader that the idea in the second sentence opposes the message of the first. Without this phrase, the two sentences would still contain contrasting information, but the passage would no longer signal to the reader that this contrast exists. The following text illustrates how this passage appears without the phrase "despite these widespread beliefs":

People who hold this belief might feel that it is useful to read comments from anyone who wants to review an item, regardless of that person's qualifications. This availability to the general public is precisely the problem with online reviews; when all people can review items, there is no guarantee that the reviewers will be knowledgeable about a product and present an unbiased opinion.

TABLE 5.2 Text Comparison from "Don't Trust Amazon.com's Customer Reviews" Excerpt

Original Text	Text with Word, Phrase, or Clause that Creates Cohesion and Clarifies Relationships Removed	Why the Word, Phrase, or Clause that Creates Cohesion and Clarifies Relationships Is Important
People who hold this belief might feel that it is useful to read comments from anyone who wants to review an item, regardless of that person's qualifications. Despite these widespread beliefs, this availability to the general public is precisely the problem with online reviews; when all people can review items, there is no guarantee that the reviewers will be knowledgeable about a product and present an unbiased opinion.	People who hold this belief might feel that it is useful to read comments from anyone who wants to review an item, regardless of that person's qualifications. This availability to the general public is precisely the problem with online reviews; when all people can review items, there is no guarantee that the reviewers will be knowledgeable about a product and present an unbiased opinion.	The phrase "despite these widespread beliefs" is important to the original text because of the way it communicates to the reader that the idea in the second sentence opposes the message of the first. The passage without this phrase lacks the same sense of flow and does not clearly indicate the contrast between the information in these sentences.

This revised example lacks the same sense of flow; the original version meets the Common Core Writing Standard of clarifying the relationship between the information in each sentence, while the new text does not. Instead, the two sentences in the revised passage seem more disjointed without the phrase "despite these widespread beliefs." Table 5.2 describes the distinctions between these two passages.

Now, let's take a look inside an eighth grade classroom and examine how these students work to understand this tool of argument writing.

A Classroom Snapshot

I begin today's class with my eighth graders with a connection between the writing strategy we've been discussing and their out-of-school lives: "I recently asked you all to be on the lookout for examples of words, phrases, and clauses that create cohesion and clarify relationships that you come across in your everyday lives. Did anyone notice any examples?"

Much to my delight, I see students around the room raise their hands. The first one I call on explains, "I heard an example when one of my friends was talking about her new iPhone. She said, 'This phone has a better camera than my last one. Plus, I get better service.'"

"Awesome," I reply. "What was the language that creates cohesion and clarifies relationships in that example?"

"It was the word 'plus,'" responds the student. "It clarifies the relationship because it shows that the two things my friend was saying about her iPhone are related. They're both reasons why she likes the phone."

"Very nice job," I say, praising her analysis. "Let's hear from someone else who noticed any examples of this language in everyday life."

I call on a student who states, "I heard my basketball coach use an example when he said, 'however.' He was talking about our next opponent and said, 'This team is undefeated this year. However, I think we can beat them.'"

"A great example," I tell the student. "How do you think the word 'however' creates cohesion and clarifies relationships in that statement?"

"It shows the differences in the sentences. The first sentence is about how good the team is. The second sentence says we can beat them. The word 'however' shows that the second sentence is going to say something different from what the first one did."

"Excellent analysis," I respond. "I love that so many of you have found examples of this writing tool in your everyday lives. As the examples that our classmates have shared show, words, phrases, and clauses that create cohesion and clarify relationships are frequently used in communication. Today, we're going to work with this writing strategy even further. You're going to work in groups and do an activity that will really help you understand why this writing strategy is so important."

In our initial conversation on this topic, these students and I looked at examples of argument essays (specifically, some of the essays featured in this book) that contain words, phrases, and clauses that create cohesion and clarify relationships between statements. Next, we discussed why these words, phrases, and clauses are important to effective argument essays. I facilitated these conversations by showing students excerpts from argument essays that contain examples of the words, phrases, and clauses that create cohesion and clarify relationships and then showing them revised versions of those excerpts that no longer contained those words, phrases, and clauses. After examining these original and revised excerpts, we discussed why the language that creates cohesion and clarifies relationships is important to the original passage.

Today, the students are doing an activity that is rooted in our last discussion, but gives them the opportunity to take on even more ownership of their learning. They will work in groups and I will give each group an excerpt from a piece of argument writing that contains language that creates cohesion and clarifies relationships. Each group will then rewrite the passage without the words, phrases, and clauses that create cohesion and clarify relationships and explain why this language is important to the original text, doing so on a chart like the one depicted in Tables 5.1 and 5.2. I describe this activity to the students and then give each group a passage from an argument essay and a chart on which to record the original text, the revised version without the language that creates cohesion and clarifies relationships, and an analysis of why this language is important to effective argument writing.

After I give each group these materials, I begin checking in with the students and monitoring their progress. I first talk with a group who are working with the following excerpt from the essay, "Smaller Classes, Successful Students":

> Walk into a classroom in a public school, and you are likely to see dedicated teachers and hard-working students. However, you are also likely to see more students crammed into each classroom than ever before. The large amount of students in each classroom is an important issue in 21st century schools: according to a 2011 *New York Times* article titled "Tight Budgets Mean Squeeze in Classrooms," funding cuts and teacher layoffs have led to increasingly more students in public school classes (Dillon, 2011). For example, this article states that a proposal in Detroit would increase high school classes to 60 students. It is imperative that schools reverse this trend and ensure small classes for their students. Small classes can maximize their students' chances of success.

"Hi you all," I say, greeting the students. "I'm excited to hear your thoughts on the words, phrases, and clauses that create cohesion and clarify relationships in this passage." The students nod and I continue: "Let's get started by thinking about what language you found in the passage that does this. What words, phrases, or clauses that create cohesion and clarify relationships did you notice?"

"We found two examples of this," responds a student in the group: "'however' in the second sentence and 'for example' in the fourth sentence."

"That's right," continues another student, "and we rewrote the paragraph without 'however' and 'for example.'"

This student proceeds to show me a revised version of this passage with "however" and "for example" omitted.

"Very nice," I tell the group. "Now, let's talk about your analysis of how this language is important. Let's start with the word 'however': why is that an important word in this passage?"

"It's important," states one student in the group, "because it shows that the essay is going to give a different kind of information. The first sentence talks about good things, like dedicated teachers and students that work hard. The second talks about not-so-good things, like overcrowded classes. The word 'however' shows that the essay is going to change from positive to negative."

"Really well said," I reply. "I love the way you identified the positive tone of the first sentence and then explained how 'however' signals a shift between that tone and a more negative one. Now, let's think about the phrase 'for example.' Why is that important to this passage?"

"That one," asserts another student, "shows that the author is going to give us specific examples of overcrowded classrooms. If the author didn't use it, the essay wouldn't be as clear because the author wouldn't show us that specific examples of overcrowded classrooms are going to be given."

"Very nice job," I tell the student. "You did very well at explaining that this phrase indicates that the author is going to provide specific examples. This is an important phrase in the essay. You all did a great job of analyzing the language in this essay that creates cohesion and clarifies relationships."

I continue to circulate around the classroom, checking in with each small group. I continue to be impressed by each group's analysis of the significance of the words, phrases, and clauses that create cohesion and clarify relationships. "All of you did really well at this," I tell the class. "When we next meet, we're going to focus on using these words, phrases, and clauses that create cohesion and clarify relationships in your writing. Really nice work today!"

Recommendations for Teaching Students about Using Words, Phrases, and Clauses to Create Cohesion and Clarify Relationships

In this section, I describe a step-by-step instructional process to use when teaching students to use words, phrases, and clauses to create cohesion and clarify relationships in their argument writing. The instructional steps I recommend are: 1) Show students examples of words, phrases, and clauses in argument essays that create cohesion and clarify relationships, 2) Discuss with students why words, phrases, and clauses that create cohesion and clarify relationships are important tools for effective argument writing, 3) Ask students to analyze why words, phrases, and clauses that create cohesion and clarify relationships are important to examples of argument writing, 4) Have students apply the writing strategy of using words, phrases, and clauses that create cohesion and clarify relationships to their own argument essays, and 5) Help students reflect on how language that creates cohesion and clarifies relationships enhances their argument essays. Each of these recommendations is described in detail in this section.

1) Show Students Examples of Words, Phrases, and Clauses in Argument Essays that Create Cohesion and Clarify Relationships

Beginning this instructional process by showing students examples of these words, phrases, and clauses provides students with a strong foundation on which the rest of this instructional process can build. When doing this with my students, I place argument essays on the document camera and point out various words, phrases, and clauses that create cohesion and clarify relationships. While doing so, I'll also explain how this language performs its intended function; for example, if I show the students an essay containing the phrase "in addition," I'll think aloud about how "in addition" clarifies a relationship between two statements by indicating that they are about related topics. I recommend showing your students a wide range of examples of language that creates cohesion and clarifies relationships, being sure to include words, phrases, and clauses used to link similar ideas like "in addition" and "for example," as well as those used to indicate differences, such as "however" and "in contrast." Showing students these examples and discussing how they create cohesion and clarify relationships prepares students for the next step of this process—discussing why these words, phrases, and clauses are important to effective argument writing.

2) Discuss with Students Why Words, Phrases, and Clauses that Create Cohesion and Clarify Relationships Are Important Tools for Effective Argument Writing

I recommend helping students understand the importance of this concept by first showing them passages from argument writing that contain words, phrases, and clauses that create cohesion and clarify relationships, then displaying those same passages without the language that achieves this effect, and finally discussing why the language that creates cohesion and clarifies relationships is important to making the piece as strong as possible. This activity builds off of the first step of the instructional process, as it goes beyond showing students examples of this concept and helps them understand its significance to effective argument writing. When doing this with my students, I use a chart like the one depicted in Tables 5.1 and 5.2 (and available in Appendix B) that places the original and revised text next to each other and also provides a space to record the differences between these two texts. The juxtaposition of these passages helps emphasize why the writing strategy of using words, phrases, and clauses that create cohesion and clarify relationships is important to effective argument writing: this writing tool clearly communicates how statements and ideas in an essay relate to one another and makes a piece easier to comprehend.

Earlier in this chapter, we looked at excerpts from the argument essays "The Importance of Baseball" and "Don't Trust Amazon.com Customer Reviews," examining how those passages differ without the words, phrases, or clauses the author used to create cohesion and clarify relationships. When doing this with your students, you can use these essays or any others in Appendix A of this book to help students understand the importance of this argument writing tool. I recommend showing students an example of how a passage looks with and without this language and thinking aloud about why the words, phrases, and clauses that create cohesion and clarify relationships are important. I suggest then involving students a bit more in the process by asking them to help identify the language that creates cohesion and clarifies relationships and share their thoughts regarding why this language is important to the original passage. This makes the activity increasingly interactive and gives teachers insight into how well the students are grasping the concept.

3) Ask Students to Analyze Why Words, Phrases, and Clauses that Create Cohesion and Clarify Relationships Are Important to Examples of Argument Writing

The next step of this instructional process is for students to take an even more active role in analyzing the importance of this argument writing tool by asking them to identify language that creates cohesion and clarifies relationships and then analyze the significance of that language. This activity, an example of which is described in this chapter's classroom snapshot, is an even more student-focused version of the previous instructional recommendation, in which the teacher leads a discussion with students about why language that creates cohesion and clarifies relationships is significant to effective argument writing. To conduct this student-centered activity in your classroom, give students excerpts from argument writing that contain words, phrases, and clauses that create cohesion and clarify relationships as well as templates of the chart depicted in Tables 5.1 and 5.2. (You can have students work on this activity in small groups or independently.) Ask the students to first identify the language that creates cohesion and clarifies relationships, then rewrite the passage without that language, and lastly analyze why the words, phrases, and clauses that perform this function are important to the original passage.

As the students do this, circulate around the room and check in with them, as I did in the classroom snapshot. When you meet with the students or groups, focus on whether they've identified the language in the text that creates cohesion and clarifies relationships and how well they've analyzed the importance of this language. The group described in the classroom snapshot did a great job of identifying "however" and "for example" as examples of language that performs this function and describing why their use makes the original passage as effective as possible. If students are struggling with their analysis, ask them to consider what role the identified language plays in the original text and how the new text reads differently without these words, phrases, or clauses. These probing questions can help students think about the importance of this argument writing tool.

4) Have Students Apply the Writing Strategy of Using Words, Phrases, and Clauses that Create Cohesion and Clarify Relationships to Their Own Argument Essays

The next step of this instructional process gives even more ownership to the students, asking them to apply the writing strategy of using language that creates cohesion and clarifies relationships to their works. Applying this writing strategy to their own essays allows students to use it to enhance works that are personally relevant and meaningful to them, increasing the relevance of the lesson and the students' levels of engagement (Ladson-Billings, 1995). When asking your students to apply this strategy to their works, I recommend instructing them to do the following: 1) Examine your existing work, looking for places where ideas could be more clearly connected, 2) Add appropriate words, phrases, and clauses to create cohesion between these ideas and clarify relationships, 3) Continue writing your argument essay, being on the lookout for places to use words, phrases, and clauses that create cohesion and clarify relationships.

While the students work, I suggest conferring with them and monitoring how well they are putting this writing strategy into practice. I recently spoke with a student who explained that he enhanced his argument essay by adding language that clarifies relationships to its introduction. "I'm writing about why we shouldn't spend so much time on standardized tests in school," he explained, "and I added 'in addition' and 'because of this' to connect the ideas I wrote about. I also added the word 'instead' before the last sentence, when I say what I think schools should do in place of spending all this time on standardized tests." The essay excerpt to which this student refers is depicted in Figure 5.1.

Figure 5.1 Student Work Example Containing Language that Creates Cohesion and Clarifies Relationships

Since the No Child Left Behind Law was passed in 2001 (U.S. Department of Education, 2015), standardized testing has been a big part of life in America's public schools. These tests are used to measure how well teachers, schools, districts, and states are teaching their students and preparing them for college and careers (U.S. Department of Education, 2015). In my school, students spend a whole lot of time getting ready for these tests. We take a bunch of practice tests and talk about test taking strategies. In addition, we spend a lot of school time taking the tests instead of learning new things. Because of this, I believe schools should not have students spend as much time getting ready for and taking standardized tests. Instead, schools should have students spend that time learning new and interesting things.

This student's work exhibits his understanding of this writing tool; the use of "in addition," "because of this," and "instead" gives his work a sense of cohesion it would not otherwise have.

5) Help Students Reflect on How Language that Creates Cohesion and Clarifies Relationships Enhances Their Argument Essays

I like to conclude this instructional process by helping students reflect on how this argument writing tool has enhanced their own pieces. To facilitate these reflections, I recommend asking students to respond to the following questions: "How would your essay be different without words, phrases, and clauses that create cohesion and clarify relationships?" and "How does the use of these words, phrases, and clauses enhance your essay?" These related questions call for students to consider the significance of this writing strategy to their own works, maximizing their awareness of its importance to effective argument writing. The student who wrote the previously discussed piece on standardized tests explained his work would be different without this writing tool "because my statements just wouldn't connect to each other as well. They'd feel much more disconnected." He continued to say that this strategy enhances his essay "because the essay would be much harder to understand without words and phrases like the ones I used that connect ideas." This awareness of the importance of words, phrases, and clauses that create cohesion and link ideas indicates this student's understanding of the impact this writing strategy can have on a piece of argument writing.

Final Thoughts on Using Words, Phrases, and Clauses to Create Cohesion and Clarify Relationships

- ◆ Using words, phrases, and clauses to create cohesion and clarify relationships is addressed in Common Core Writing Standards W.6.1.C, W.7.1.C, and W.8.1.C.
- ◆ Authors of argument essays use certain words, phrases, and clauses to connect the ideas in their works and show the ways these ideas relate to one another.
  - ◆ If an author is connecting similar ideas, she might use language like "for example," "in addition," "another," and "because," as all of these examples can link related points.
  - ◆ If an author wants to show that two ideas are dissimilar in some way, she might use "however," "in contrast," or "despite this" to call the reader's attention to these differences.
- ◆ The writing strategy of using words, phrases, and clauses to create cohesion and clarify relationships is important to

effective argument writing because it clearly communicates to readers how statements and ideas relate to one another.

- ◆ When teaching students about using words, phrases, and clauses to create cohesion and clarify relationships:
  - ◆ Show students examples of words, phrases, and clauses in argument essays that create cohesion and clarify relationships.
  - ◆ Discuss with students why words, phrases, and clauses that create cohesion and clarify relationships are important tools for effective argument writing.
  - ◆ Ask students to analyze why words, phrases, and clauses that create cohesion and clarify relationships are important to examples of argument writing.
  - ◆ Have students apply the writing strategy of using words, phrases, and clauses that create cohesion and clarify relationships to their own argument essays.
  - ◆ Help students reflect on how language that creates cohesion and clarifies relationships enhances their argument essays.

6

Establishing and
Maintaining a Formal Style

What Does "Establishing and Maintaining a Formal Style" Mean?

An effective argument essay is not only characterized by the quality of the information the author presents, but also the style the author uses when doing so. Specifically, strong argument writers use a formal style consistent with the reader's expectations for an argument essay. The Common Core Writing Standards highlight the importance of this concept—Standards W.6.1.D, W.7.1.D, and W.8.1.D call for students to "establish and maintain a formal style" in their argument writing (Common Core State Standards Initiative, 2010). In this chapter, we'll explore the following: what "establishing and maintaining a formal style" means, why using this strategy is important to effective argument writing, an example of a lesson that helps students understand this strategy, and key recommendations for helping your students establish and maintain a formal style in their own argument writing. While examining these topics, we'll take a look at excerpts from argument essays that utilize this writing tool.

First, let's think about what it means to establish and maintain a formal style. Formal writing adheres to the conventions of Edited American English—English without regional or cultural variations (Kolln & Funk, 2009) that appeals to the widest audience possible. When I talk with my students about writing in a formal style, I explain to them that the language choices we make when we write are shaped by a piece's audience, purpose, and corresponding language expectation. For example, a text message a student writes to a friend about their weekend plans is likely to have an informal language expectation because it is about an informal topic and written to someone that the author knows well. Similarly, a

Facebook post about one's recent vacation also has informal language expectations, since it addresses an informal topic and is conveyed to an audience of people the writer knows.

In contrast, an argument essay has more formal language expectations because of its audience and purpose. Argument writers typically write for a "universal audience" (Perelman & Olbrechts-Tyteca, 1969), meaning they are presenting their ideas, reasons, and evidence to anyone who encounters their work. This concept is especially important for students who want to share their ideas with a broad audience, such as people in one's community or others who are interested in a particular issue (like the student we met in Chapter 3 who created a blog to share his ideas about preserving the health of young athletes). When students write for a universal audience, they need to use formal language to ensure all readers will understand their ideas. In addition, the purpose of argument writing also aligns with formal language: argument writers present evidence-based claims about which they feel strongly, and do so with the intention of convincing others to adopt similar beliefs. The seriousness of this purpose aligns with formal language, as formal language helps an author be well-received by as wide an audience as possible.

To illustrate the role of formal language in argument writing, let's take a look at an excerpt from the argument essay "Schools Should Stay Away from Computer Grading":

> Some proponents of computer grading point out the way it gives students faster evaluations than hand-graded essays and contend that this immediate feedback would benefit students. For example, Anant Agarwal, the president of an organization called edX that offers courses online, is quoted in a *New York Times* article on this topic as saying, "There is a huge value in learning with instant feedback" (Markoff, 2013). However, despite any benefits associated with immediate feedback, the problems with computer grading are more significant, such as Les Perelman's previously mentioned research findings on the inaccuracies of computer grading programs. Another problem that outweighs the benefits of computer grading relates to the knowledge that teachers have of their students and those students' abilities. Writing-instruction experts Ralph Fletcher and Joann Portalupi (2001) explain that a key component of providing useful feedback to student writers is the teacher's understanding of that student. A computer grading program cannot possess this same type of awareness.

This passage's use of formal language aligns with its audience and purpose; it is written in Edited American English to help it appeal to a universal audience and uses this language and experts' opinions to make it as convincing as possible. If the author were writing to a different audience or about a different topic, he might use less formal language or rely less on expert evidence and insights to support his claim. However, given the nature of argument writing, the formal tone of this passage is best suited to the genre. In our next section, we'll further examine why using a formal style is an important component of effective argument writing.

Why Establishing and Maintaining a Formal Style Is Important to Effective Argument Writing

I recently spoke with a middle schooler who was curious about the importance of this writing strategy. "Can you explain this to me?" she asked. "I know what a formal style is, but I don't think I understand why it's important to argument writing."

"Absolutely," I responded. "I'm going to make a comparison to clothes. Someone might have a lot of different kinds of clothes in his or her closet. Some might be for playing sports, some might be for going out with friends, and some might be for dressing up. What would happen if an occasion called for someone to dress up and he or she wore sports clothes instead?"

"It would look weird," replied the student.

"Right," I affirmed. "And if you were giving a speech and wearing formal clothes, and someone else was giving a speech and wearing gym shorts and a t-shirt, would the audience take both of you as seriously?"

"No," she answered. "They would take me more seriously because I dressed how I did."

"Exactly," I stated. "You dressed appropriately for the situation. I wouldn't wear my gym clothes to teach, and I wouldn't wear dress clothes and a tie to go to the gym. Just like these different kinds of clothes, different kinds of language are all valuable and important, they just are best used in different situations. Writing an argument essay like you're writing a text message to a friend would seem odd, just like it might seem odd if you used formal language in that text message."

As I explained to this student, formal language is not better than any other form of language, but it does most align with the expectations of argument writing. An argument writer who uses formal language will be taken as seriously as possible by his or her audience, just like someone giving a speech will be taken as seriously as possible if his or her attire matches the occasion. An argument essay with strong ideas but without the effective use of formal language will not be as effective as one that utilizes this language form well. In addition, an essay that uses formal language will be easily understood by as many people as possible, while one that uses slang or informal language may not.

To illustrate these ideas, let's compare the previously described passage from "Schools Should Stay Away from Computer Grading" with

TABLE 6.1 Formal and Informal Language Versions of "Schools Should Stay Away from Computer Grading" Excerpt

Original Formal Version	Revised Informal Version	Why the Formal Language Is Important to the Original Passage
However, despite any benefits associated with immediate feedback, the problems with computer grading are more significant, such as Les Perelman's previously mentioned research findings on the inaccuracies of computer grading programs. Another problem that outweighs the benefits of computer grading relates to the knowledge that teachers have of their students and those students' abilities.	There's still a bunch of stuff wrong with computer grading, like the whole thing about them not being accurate and the way teachers know info about their students that computers don't. These things show that computer grading is pretty lame.	The formal language used in the original passage suggests that the author takes this topic seriously. For example, the language "despite any benefits associated with immediate feedback, the problems with computer grading are more significant" sends a much more serious message than "there's still a bunch of stuff wrong with computer grading." The formal language communicates to readers that the author has thought carefully about this topic and the way he wants to communicate his ideas about it. The formal language can also be understood by as many people as possible. The informal version might not be as clear to as many readers because informal words like "lame" might not be easily understood by everyone reading.

how it might look if it was written in informal language. Table 6.1 juxtaposes a selection from this passage with an informal version of it and explains why the formal language is important to the original passage (a template for this figure is available in Appendix B).

As the explanation in the third column indicates, formal language is important to the original passage because it suggests that the author has thought carefully about this topic and takes it seriously and uses language that is understood by a general audience. If an author shows that she has given a topic a great deal of careful consideration, readers will be more likely to value her perspective. In contrast, if an author sends a message that she hasn't done much in-depth thinking about an issue, readers are more likely to dismiss her argument. By encouraging our students to use formal language when they write argument essays, we teachers can help them be taken as seriously as possible by their readers and to ensure their ideas are understood by a wide range of readers. Now, let's take a look inside an eighth grade classroom and examine how the students in this class explore the importance of formal language to effective argument writing.

A Classroom Snapshot

Today's class begins with one of those moments that reminds me how much I love teaching; a student raises her hand and says, "I think this whole thing about formal language is really interesting. This is the first time I've ever thought about why formal language is important to argument writing. Now I can see why using formal language is good for argument writing and important."

Grinning widely, I respond to her statement: "I'm so glad to hear this. The use of formal language is definitely a key tool for effective argument writing. I love that you're finding it interesting."

"Yeah," replies the student. "It's like, teachers have told me before to write in formal language, but I never thought before about *why* to do it."

"I love that you're thinking about that now," I say, thrilled by the student's metacognitive awareness of this concept. In our last class, these students and I discussed the importance of formal language to effective argument writing; we examined excerpts from argument essays (written in their original, formal language), compared them to revised versions written in informal language, and then discussed why the use of formal language is important to the effectiveness of the original excerpt. Today, we're going to do an activity that is similar in some ways, but also gives more ownership and responsibility to the students: I will divide the students into groups and give each group an excerpt from an argument essay, as well as a template for the chart depicted in Table 6.1. Each group will be responsible for "translating" its assigned excerpt into informal language and then analyzing why the use of formal language is important to the original passage. This activity is designed to further increase the students' awareness of the importance of using formal language in argument writing by helping them understand the different impacts argument essays in formal and informal language can have on readers.

After I introduce the activity to the students and assign them to groups, I give each group an essay excerpt and a template. "I think you all will do a great job with this," I tell them. "To get started, read the excerpt I gave you. Once you've finished reading it, talk with your group members about what the excerpt could look like in informal language and write that down in the appropriate column. Finally, talk with your group members about why you think the formal language is important to the original passage and write your analysis in the final column. While you work, I'll move around the room and talk with each group."

I check in with a group working with the following excerpt from the argument essay "Lower the Cost of College":

> Some people oppose efforts to decrease college costs, asserting that making colleges cheaper for students will require the government to spend money to offset the lower tuition amounts that the colleges receive and that the government cannot afford to do so. While the government may need to spend money for college costs to decrease, there are a number of ways that having a highly educated and debt-free population can positively impact society. Young people in a great deal of debt can't purchase many things, which hurts the economy. If recent college graduates are concerned with paying off their loans and not purchasing houses and cars, the housing and auto industries may decline. However, these and other businesses may thrive if young people are not overcome with debt. Also, a country with more well-educated people contains more individuals who can produce innovations, ideas, and products that can bring profit to the country's industries and create jobs. If the government invests in helping students graduate debt-free from college, these promising possibilities may become reality.

"Hi there," I say to the group. "Tell me how things are going so far." "Real well," shares one student. "This is fun—we had fun turning this into informal language."

"I'm thrilled to hear it," I respond. "Let's have someone read the original, formal version out loud and then read the revised, informal version."

"I'll do it," volunteers a student in the group. She first reads the original version and then shares the informal version the group created:

> Some peeps say that college should still cost a ton of money because they think it's better to have it like that than for the government to go broke. Whatevs, people. The government isn't gonna go broke because it's awesomesauce for society if young people don't have debt! This is because people who aren't in debt can spend mad money. Plus, if more people can go to college, we'll have even more smart people, and that's awesome because they can come up with more sweet products, like the next iPhone!

"I love it," I praise the students, laughing with delight at their expressive informal language. "You all did a wonderful job of using informal language and making the revised version of this passage your own. There's definitely a different feel in this new version! Now, let's think about why the formal language is important to the original passage. Why do you all think it's important?"

"It definitely would make someone reading the essay take it more seriously than if it had the informal language we used," responds a student in the group.

"Yeah," interjects another. "The language we used is what you might say with your friends, but you wouldn't use it if you wanted to be taken seriously when you're writing about something important."

"And," adds another student, "not everyone would understand the informal language. Some people might not know what things like 'mad money' and 'awesomesauce' mean. Formal language is understood by more people."

"Very well said," I tell the students. "These two language forms are used for different purposes—one to be casual and informal, such as with friends, and the other to be taken seriously and widely understood by an audience. Excellent analysis!"

I check in with the groups in the class and am pleased that each group has done a wonderful job translating its passage to informal language and then analyzing the differences. "Wonderful work, all of you," I tell them. "You did a great job of thinking about the importance of formal language to argument writing. Remember, both formal and informal language are valuable and important ways to communicate—they simply are aligned with different purposes. To get your point across as effectively as possible to a wide audience, you'll want to use formal language in your argument writing."

Recommendations for Teaching Students about Establishing and Maintaining a Formal Style

In this section, I describe a step-by-step instructional process to use when teaching students about establishing and maintaining a formal style in argument writing. The instructional steps I recommend are: 1) Show students mentor examples of argument essays that use formal language, 2) Talk with students about the importance of formal language to effective argument writing, 3) Have students analyze why formal language strengthens argument writing, 4) Ask students to apply formal language to their own argument writing, and 5) Help students reflect on why the use of formal language enhances their own argument essays. Each of these recommendations is addressed in detail in this section.

1) Show Students Mentor Examples of Argument Essays that Use Formal Language

Showing students examples of argument essays written in formal language has two key benefits: 1) It clarifies for students what formal language looks like, and 2) It teaches students that argument writing is an occasion to code-switch to formal language. It's important to provide examples of how formal language looks and sounds so that students have clear under-standings of this concept. While some students might come to middle school with clear understandings of what formal language looks and sounds like, others may not, as formal language differs from the home languages spoken by some students (Wheeler & Swords, 2006). I recom-mend emphasizing to students that all language forms are valuable and important; respecting students' home dialects leads to a culturally inclu-sive classroom (Wheeler & Swords, 2006). An especially effective way to value students' home languages and dialects is discussing code-switching, in which writers and speakers move from one linguistic style to another. Students who can code-switch to formal language can use this writing style in their argument essays. Once students understand the features of formal English, they can move to the next step of this instruc-tional process, which focuses on the importance of this language form to effective argument writing.

2) Talk with Students about the Importance of Formal Language to Effective Argument Writing

I like to facilitate discussions with my students about the significance of this argument writing strategy by juxtaposing an argument essay written in formal language with a revised version of the essay that uses informal language instead. I then talk with students about why formal language is important to the original essay, focusing on the way formal language ensures a reader's ideas will be taken as seriously as possible and will be easily understood by a wide audience. In contrast, I tell my students, an essay written informally and in slang that is not understood by as wide an audience will not be as credible or clear to as many readers.

When doing this with your students, I recommend copying the tem-plate of Table 6.1 available in Appendix B and filling it out with an excerpt from a formal version of an argument essay (such as a section from an essay in Appendix A), your own informal version of that excerpt, and then your analysis of why the formal language enhances the original text. In your analysis, cite specific words and phrases in the original text that maximize the piece's credibility and readability. Once you've done this, place the form on a document camera and discuss it with your students. Next, fill out a new form with an excerpt from another formal essay and an informal version of that excerpt, but leave the final column (which asks why formal language is important to the original text) blank. Then, read both versions with the students and ask for their feedback when completing this last column. This procedure releases responsibility to the students and helps you evaluate their awareness of the importance of this writing tool. After I recently conducted this lesson in a middle school, a student told me that she liked the increasing responsibility this lesson provides: "It was helpful how you showed us how to write about why formal language is important before asking us to answer that question. It helped me understand what to do."

3) Have Students Analyze Why Formal Language Strengthens Argument Writing

I recommend following the preceding discussion of the importance of formal language to effective argument by asking students to work in small groups or individually to do their own revision and analysis of a formally written argument essay. In this activity, an example of which is described in this chapter's classroom snapshot, the teacher gives each student or group an excerpt from an argument essay written in formal language and asks each group to revise the excerpt so it's no longer written in formal language and then analyze why formal language is important to the original version of the essay. I've found that this activity is both enjoyable and informative for students: they typically have fun changing the formally written excerpt to an informal version (such as the students in the classroom snapshot who used contemporary slang terms "whatevs" and "awesomesauce" in their adaptation) and they benefit from critiquing why formal language is an important strategy for effective argument writing.

A middle school English teacher who did this activity with her class explained to me that her students had similar experiences: "This was definitely fun for my kids. One group changed an essay about making school start later to include language like 'ballin'' and 'btw,' which are both things they say when they're being informal. They had fun with that, and they definitely learned why formal language is important too." I suggest circulating around the room and conferring with students as they work on this activity; this can ensure that your students are effectively translating text from formal to informal English and that they're understanding the significance of formal language to effective argument writing. If a student or group is struggling with the importance of this concept, I suggest drawing comparisons to other context-specific choices, such as different clothes that align with different purposes. This can help emphasize to students that both language forms are valuable, but formal language is best aligned with argument writing.

4) Ask Students to Apply Formal Language to Their Own Argument Writing

The first three steps of this instructional process have asked students to take increasing responsibility for their learning—starting with teacher-found examples, moving to a class discussion of the importance of this writing strategy, and then transitioning to an activity that asks students to analyze the strategy themselves. The fourth step gives students even more ownership, as it calls for students to apply the argument writing tool of using formal language to their own works. I recommend telling students that there are two components of putting this strategy into practice: 1) They can review argument writing they've already done and make sure they've used formal language, and 2) They can be sure to use formal language as they continue working on their argument essays. Once you've explained these methods, ask your students to apply them to their own works and hold one-on-one conferences with them as they do so.

During these conferences, I begin by asking students if they noticed any informal language that they changed to formal language. Next, I'll ask them to point out some formal language in their essays. I held a conference on the use of formal language with a middle schooler who was writing about the idea that students' textbooks should be downloaded on e-readers. The student explained that he noticed some informal language he used that should be changed to formal language: "In my first draft, I used some informal language when talking about the features of e-readers. I said that some of the features of Kindles are 'sweet,' but I realized that it would be better to change that word to something more formal sounding, like 'innovative' or 'appealing.'" I'll then conclude the conference by taking a look at the students' essays to see if there is any informal language they used but didn't notice. If so, I'll ask students to read that section aloud—this typically helps them identify the informal language. These steps and procedures allow us teachers to evaluate how well our students are applying this argument writing tool to their works.

5) Help Students Reflect on Why the Use of Formal Language Enhances Their Own Argument Essays

This final step requires students to consider the importance of formal language to the argument essays they've created. Concluding the instructional process in this way helps students reflect on why formal language is a tool that make their works as effective as possible. While the students have already considered the importance of formal language to argument writing in general, this activity makes the connection between the focal strategy and students' *own* writing, increasing its relevance and applicability. To help students reflect on the significance of this concept, I suggest posing the following questions: 1) How would your argument essay be different if you didn't use formal language? and 2) How does the use of formal language enhance your argument essay? These related questions are designed to help students think metacognitively about how the use of formal language makes their argument writing as strong as possible.

The student whose thoughts on this concept are featured in the previous recommendation responded to these questions by highlighting the importance of formal language to his essay about e-readers: "If I didn't use formal language, my main ideas would still be basically the same, but my essay wouldn't be as effective. It would be harder for a lot of people to understand some of my points if I used slang words. Using formal language makes it so that more people can understand my essay and will take it seriously." This student makes an excellent point when explaining that the use of formal or informal language doesn't impact the main ideas of his essay, but does impact the ways those ideas are conveyed to readers. As he explains, readers are more likely to understand his ideas and take them seriously when he uses formal language.

Final Thoughts on Establishing and Maintaining a Formal Style

- ◆ Establishing and maintaining a formal style is addressed in Common Core Writing Standards W.6.1.D, W.7.1.D, and W.8.1.D.
- ◆ Formal writing adheres to the conventions of Edited American English.
- ◆ The language choices we make when we write are shaped by a piece's audience, purpose, and corresponding language expectation—the universal audience and serious purpose of argument writing result in a formal language expectation.
- ◆ The use of formal language in argument writing ensures a reader's ideas will be taken as seriously as possible and will be easily understood by a wide audience.
- ◆ All language forms are valuable and important.
- ◆ Different language varieties are best suited to different situations.
- ◆ Formal language is the variety best suited to argument writing.
- ◆ When teaching students about establishing and maintaining a formal style:
    - ◆ Show students mentor examples of argument essays that use formal language.
    - ◆ Talk with students about the importance of formal language to effective argument writing.
    - ◆ Have students analyze why formal language strengthens argument writing.
    - ◆ Ask students to apply formal language to their own argument writing.
    - ◆ Help students reflect on why the use of formal language enhances their own argument essays.

7

Creating an Effective Concluding Section

What Does "Creating an Effective Concluding Section" Mean?

During a recent conversation with a middle school language arts teacher, I was reminded that an argument essay cannot achieve its maximum effectiveness without a strong concluding section. "My students are really loving argument writing and doing a great job of it, with one exception," he explained. "They really need help with conclusions. Their conclusions are either nonexistent or are really brief summaries of things they've already said." This teacher's comment calls attention to the importance of effective conclusions to argument writing and the challenges some students experience when creating them. The Common Core State Standards also identify the significance of this concept, as Standards W.6.1.E, W.7.1.E, and W.8.1.E highlight its importance. In this chapter, we'll discuss the following ideas related to crafting strong conclusions in argument writing: what "creating an effective concluding section" means, why effective conclusions are important to quality argument writing, a description of a lesson on this concept, and key recommendations for helping your students create effective conclusions in their own works.

First, let's consider what it means to create an effective concluding section. As the teacher in the previous paragraph pointed out, conclusions should do more than provide a brief summary of previously stated information. An effective conclusion provides a sense of closure to a piece of writing, while a conclusion that simply restates previous points doesn't do anything to enhance the quality of a piece (Zinsser, 2006). A strong concluding section to an argument essay should do the following: 1) Emphasize the significance of the cause for which the essay is arguing, and 2) Leave readers with a final thought about the piece's claim. Let's examine these attributes in the conclusion to "Keep Gym Class in Schools," which reads:

> Gym class is an important part of the school curriculum that, according to research, helps maximize student success. In today's high-stakes-testing environment and increasingly innovative world, our students need as much support as possible. Keeping gym class in school is an opportunity to help students achieve high academic goals while also contributing to the health of our country's youth. These academic and health benefits can positively impact our society in a number of ways, ranging from more students attending college to fewer health problems among children. So, if anyone ever asks if you believe gym class is important, say "Yes! It keeps our young people fit and intelligent—a great combination!"

In this concluding paragraph, the author emphasizes the significance of keeping gym class in today's schools by calling attention to the "high-stakes-testing environment and increasingly innovative world" in which we live, as well as research findings that indicate the connection between fitness and academic performance. In addition, the author successfully leaves readers with a final thought regarding the piece's claim, noting how the "academic and health benefits" of gym class can have positive impacts on societal issues such as college attendance and children's health. Table 7.1 identifies the important actions of an argument essay's conclusion and specific aspects of the conclusion to "Keep Gym Class in Schools"

TABLE 7.1 Key Actions of an Argument Essay's Conclusion

Key Actions	Excerpt from "Keep Gym Class in Schools" that Performs These Actions
1. Emphasize the significance of the cause for which the essay is arguing	Gym class is an important part of the school curriculum that, according to research, helps maximize student success. In today's high-stakes-testing environment and increasingly innovative world, our students need as much support as possible.
2. Leave readers with a final thought about the piece's claim	Keeping gym class in school is an opportunity to help students achieve high academic goals while also contributing to the health of our country's youth. These academic and health benefits can positively impact our society in a number of ways, ranging from more students attending college to fewer health problems among children.

that perform them (a reproducible template of this chart can be found in Appendix B).

Why Creating an Effective Conclusion Is Important to Strong Argument Writing

One of my middle school students recently shared an observation in the class that nicely highlighted the importance of creating an effective conclusion: "I want to be a lawyer someday and I love watching movies and TV shows about lawyers. I was watching one of these movies yesterday and the main lawyer character spent a bunch of time preparing for his closing argument. Conclusions in argument essays are kind of like that closing argument."

I love the connection this student made between conclusion writing and a topic in which he is very interested. As he explained, closing arguments in court cases have key similarities to conclusions in argument essays. In both cases, someone has already presented a claim and evidence meant to support it, and is now presenting a final statement designed to make an argument as effective as possible. Just as lawyers' cases would feel incomplete without closing arguments, an argument essay wouldn't seem complete without a concluding paragraph. In addition, both closing arguments and concluding paragraphs are at their strongest if they go beyond basic summaries, instead emphasizing the significance of the cause for which they're arguing and highlighting final thoughts with which to leave others. In this section, we'll examine why each of these key actions are important to effective concluding paragraphs to argument essays.

Emphasize the Significance of the Cause for Which the Essay Is Arguing

I don't want to finish reading an argument essay and say to myself, "That topic didn't strike me as very important—I'm not sure why I just spent time reading an essay about it." Instead, I want to feel that I just read about a very important cause that is worth my time and consideration. Argument authors can help readers feel that they have read about a meaningful topic by emphasizing its significance in the conclusion. We teachers can help our students maximize the effectiveness of their conclusions by explaining to them that one of the jobs of a conclusion is to highlight the importance of the piece's claim. Specific ways of emphasizing this importance may vary somewhat depending on an essay's topic, but an effective general strategy I share with my students is the "so what?" requirement. A conclusion that meets this requirement emphasizes important points related to the essay's cause that readers are likely to care about, such as the connection between gym class and students' academic success discussed in the essay "Keep Gym Class in Schools." This connection answers the question "so what?" because it highlights a reason readers should care about the author's claim. If a conclusion does not identify a

reason readers should do so, it is not likely to meet the "so what?" requirement and therefore probably doesn't emphasize the significance of the
essay's cause.

Leave Readers with a Final Thought about the Piece's Claim
An effective conclusion also leaves readers with a final thought that they
continue to consider once they've completed the piece (Zinsser, 2006). We
teachers don't want our students to write easily forgettable argument
essays; instead, we want them to create works that impact readers and
stay in their minds once they've finished. Middle school argument writers
can achieve this effect by providing readers with "big-picture" ideas to
consider, such as how a piece's claim relates to important societal issues.
I tell my students that readers might not remember specific pieces of
evidence discussed in argument essays, but they will probably recall a
strong final thought or point the author makes in the concluding paragraph. An example of a "big-picture" idea that relates to key societal
issues can be found in the concluding paragraph of "Keep Gym Class in
Schools," where the author states that gym class can increase college
attendance and decrease youth health problems. These final thoughts are
likely to linger with readers after they've completed the essay
    Now, let's take a look at the conclusion to the essay "Don't Trust
Amazon.com's Customer Reviews" and examine how it emphasizes the
significance of its cause and leaves readers with a final thought to
consider:

> If you want to know the most accurate and unbiased information
> about products you're interested in purchasing, pay attention to
> unbiased expert reviews published in reputable newspapers and
> magazines. Untrustworthy reviews on websites like Amazon.com
> have become a major problem for consumers, who can no longer
> be sure if they are reading the opinion of another honest customer
> or someone hired by a company to make a product look good and
> increase its sales. The problem of potentially dishonest internet
> reviews is a new issue in our society; before the widespread use
> of online communication, we did not have so many places to find
> out information. Now that we do, we must be very careful about
> what sources we trust.

This concluding paragraph emphasizes the significance of its cause
with the statement, "Untrustworthy reviews on websites like Amazon.
com have become a major problem for consumers, who can no longer be
sure if they are reading the opinion of another honest customer or someone hired by a company to make a product look good and increase its
sales," which satisfies the "so what?" requirement by identifying a reason
that readers should take untrustworthy Amazon.com reviews seriously.

It also leaves readers with a final thought on which to reflect by saying, "The problem of potentially dishonest internet reviews is a new issue in our society; before the widespread use of online communication, we did not have so many places to find out information. Now that we do, we must be very careful about what sources we trust." This statement connects the topic of this essay with a key societal issue—the plethora of online sources and the need to evaluate their credibility carefully. By addressing this idea, the conclusion to "Don't Trust Amazon.com's Customer Reviews" alerts readers to a "big-picture" idea likely to stay in their minds after they finish the essay.

As this conclusion illustrates, argument essays are especially effective when they emphasize the significance of the topic and leave readers with a final thought about the piece's claim. Conclusions that perform these functions go beyond basic summaries of information, identifying why the essay's cause is important and connecting its topic with an important societal issue. Now, let's take a look at how an eighth grade class works to understand the importance of strong conclusions to effective argument writing.

A Classroom Snapshot

I begin today's class on conclusions with a comparison: "I know some of you like to take things apart to really understand how they work. Last week, some of you were talking about opening up an old computer and checking out all of its different parts." Several students nod and I continue: "Opening something up and really looking at its parts is a great way to understand something. If you look under the hood of a car, you'll get a much better understanding of how it works. Today, we're going to work in small groups to do something similar with conclusions to argument essays. We're going to, in a sense, open up some conclusions and determine what makes them effective."

This is our third class meeting focusing on creating conclusions to argument essays. In our first session on this topic, I showed the students examples of effective conclusions and explained to them that strong conclusions emphasize the significance of the essay's topic and give readers a final thought about the piece's claim to consider. In our second meeting, we discussed why each of these attributes is important to a strong conclusion, examining how each is present in the conclusion to "Don't Trust Amazon.com's Customer Reviews" and discussing why the conclusion wouldn't be as strong if it didn't perform these actions.

In today's class, the students are going to do their own analysis of effective conclusions. I will divide the class into groups and give each one an essay from Appendix A of this book. "Your job," I tell the students, "is to take the conclusion to each essay and identify which part of the conclusion emphasizes the significance of the essay's cause, as well as which part provides readers with a final thought to consider once they've finished reading the essay. This will help you further understand the features of strong conclusions and why they're important, just like opening up a computer or looking under the hood of a car could help you understand those things."

"To help you do this, I'm going to give each group a chart to fill out," I tell the students, putting the template version of Table 7.1 on the document camera. "The left side of this chart identifies the key actions a conclusion performs, while the right side asks for you to identify the sentences in an essay's conclusion that perform each of these actions."

A number of students in the class nod; one states, "I see what you mean about looking under the hoods of these conclusions—we're figuring out how they work."

"Exactly!" I exclaim. "You're definitely figuring out how they work! By looking carefully at an essay's conclusion and identifying which text in the conclusion performs each of these key actions, you're determining how the conclusion has the effect it has."

I give each group a template and an argument essay and walk around the classroom, listening to the students discuss the features of the essays' conclusions. Once the students have taken some time to talk about the key actions of these conclusions, I begin checking in with each group and conversing with them about their findings. I sit down with a group that is working on the conclusion to "Schools Should Stay Away from Computer Grading," which reads:

Computer grading has become a popular trend in some circles, but research studies and expert opinions on writing assessment strongly advise against it. Since today's schools value rigorous standards and assessments, it is especially important that students receive accurate, high-quality feedback from teachers who know them well and are familiar with their works—features that are best provided by human grading. The conflict between human vs. computer grading raises an intriguing question with great relevance to life today—Is it better to choose a new technique because it is faster and technology-based, or is it better to choose a technique that isn't as fast but is significantly more effective? Computer grading is appealing to some because it is faster and tech-oriented, but it certainly is not the best choice for our schools and students.

"I think we've got it!" a student tells me.

"Wonderful!" I respond. "I'm ready when you are!"

The students converse briefly among themselves before a student says, "Okay, now we're definitely ready! For the part of the conclusion that emphasizes the significance of the cause, we chose this part here that says

'Since today's schools value rigorous standards and assessments, it is especially important that students receive accurate, high-quality feedback from teachers who know them well and are familiar with their works—features that are best provided by human grading.'"

"Really nice job," I reply. "Tell me why you think that section emphasizes the significance."

"Because," answers the student, "it says why getting high-quality feedback from teachers is important. It says that feedback is important because of the standards and assessments in today's schools."

"Well said," I tell the student. "That section of the conclusion definitely shows the topic's significance by explaining why it's important to today's schools. It answers the 'so what?' question we talked about in some of our previous classes. Now, how about the next key action of a conclusion? How does this conclusion leave readers with a final thought about the piece's claim?"

"It does that right here," says another student in the group, "where it says 'The conflict between human vs. computer grading raises an intriguing question with great relevance to life today—Is it better to choose a new technique because it is faster and technology-based, or is it better to choose a technique that isn't as fast but is significantly more effective? Computer grading is appealing to some because it is faster and tech-oriented, but it certainly is not the best choice for our schools and students.' We thought that part leaves the readers with a final thought because it gives them something else to think about. It makes them think about whether it's best to use a faster technique that includes technology, or one that isn't fast but works better."

"Awesome job," I praise the student. "That's an excellent analysis. I love how you talked about the way this section of the conclusion gives readers something else to think about. This part of the conclusion definitely gives readers a 'big-picture' idea to consider—whether newer, faster, things are always better. You did a wonderful job of pointing that out."

I thank these students for their excellent work and continue to move around the room, speaking with other groups about their analyses. Like the first group, the other students also provide excellent explanations of how the conclusions they're analyzing emphasize the significance of a piece's cause and provide readers with thoughtful final points to consider.

"I'm so proud of all you on your analyses of these conclusions," I tell the students. "I love the way you identified specific excerpts from the texts that perform each of the key functions of a conclusion, as well as the way you described how these excerpts do so. Tomorrow, we're going to put these ideas into action by applying them to our own conclusions—I can't wait to see what you do!"

Recommendations for Teaching Students about Creating an Effective Concluding Section

In this section, I describe a step-by-step instructional process to use when teaching students about creating effective conclusions in argument writing. The instructional steps I recommend are: 1) Show students examples of strong conclusions to argument essays and discuss the features of those conclusions, 2) Discuss with students why strong conclusions are important to effective argument writing, 3) Ask students to analyze why the features of strong conclusions are important, 4) Work with students as they craft conclusions to their own argument essays, and 5) Have students reflect on why their conclusions are important to their own argument writing. Each of these recommendations is described in detail in this section.

1) Show Students Examples of Strong Conclusions to Argument Essays and Discuss the Features of Those Conclusions

Showing students examples of effective conclusions provides them with concrete examples of how this writing strategy looks in practice and facilitates conversations about the attributes those examples possess. When I present strong conclusions from argument essays to my students, I put an example on a document camera and read it out loud, asking them to follow along. Next, I explain that an effective conclusion should emphasize the significance of the cause for which its essay is arguing and leave readers with a final thought about the piece's claim; I then identify specific ways the conclusion I've shared contains these attributes.

For example, when recently working with an eighth grade class on this concept, I showed the students the conclusion from the argument essay "Keep Gym Class in Schools" previously described in this chapter, and pointed out specific ways the conclusion emphasizes the significance of physical education while also leaving readers with a final, "big-picture" thought about how keeping gym class in schools can address important societal issues such as college attendance and youth health problems. When showing your students an example of a conclusion, remember to identify specific ways the piece incorporates the key features of a strong concluding section; this will maximize the students' understandings of how authors achieve these results.

2) Discuss with Students Why Strong Conclusions Are Important to Effective Argument Writing

This instructional step helps students comprehend why the features of a strong conclusion can enhance a reader's experience. When I discuss with students why effective conclusions are important to exemplary argument writing, I focus on the reasons that highlighting the significance of an essay's cause and leaving readers with a final thought on the topic are key actions of a strong conclusion; this gets the students thinking metacognitively about these attributes, which is one of my main instructional goals. When I talk with students about a particular writing tool or strategy, I don't want them to simply do something in their writing because I've told them to; I want them to do it because they have the metacognitive awareness of why that strategy will make their work effective.

In a recent conversation with a group of eighth graders on this topic, I showed the students a number of argument essay conclusions and talked with them about why it is important that the conclusions were crafted so effectively. One example we discussed was the conclusion from the essay "Introverts Can Be Great Leaders, Too," which reads:

> Schools, employers, community organizations, and others charged with appointing individuals to leadership positions should take into account the varied personalities that effective leaders can have. Those who dismiss the idea that both introverts and extroverts can be effective leaders may overlook very talented people. It would be very unfortunate if leaders such as Bill Gates, Mother Theresa, and Abraham Lincoln were not given opportunities because of their introverted natures. The idea that individuals with a range of personalities can effectively lead also speaks to an overarching societal issue: common perceptions of who should hold certain roles can be very limiting. We should reconsider assumptions and be aware of different ways people can display abilities and perform tasks effectively.

After showing students this concluding paragraph, I explained that the author emphasizes the significance of the essay's cause by pointing out that those who dismiss introverts' leadership potential may overlook talented and effective leaders, as well as by using specific examples of introverts who have held important leadership roles. I also discussed how the author of this conclusion leaves readers with a final thought about this topic by addressing how people should reconsider commonly held perceptions and assumptions. I then talked with the students about the impact this conclusion has on the entire essay: "This conclusion is really important to the success of the whole essay. It emphasizes the importance of the essay's topic and leaves readers with a 'big-picture' final thought to consider. If this conclusion wasn't so strong, readers might not be as convinced of the topic's significance or finish with any overarching final thoughts to consider. With it, they definitely do."

3)   Ask Students to Analyze Why the Features of Strong
      Conclusions Are Important

I recommend following up on the discussions described in step two of
this instructional process by giving students more ownership of their
learning; this ownership comes from asking students to work individually
or in small groups to identify an argument essay's conclusion and analyze
how it meets the criteria for effective conclusions described in this chapter.
As discussed in this chapter's classroom snapshot, I recommend giving
students the template for Table 7.1 (available in Appendix B of this book)
to fill out while completing this activity; as students fill out this template,
they will need to identify specific text in an essay's conclusion that represents each of the key actions of a strong conclusion.

While students analyze conclusions and fill out these charts, I like to
meet with them and ask them to justify their decisions, using questions
like "Why do you think this section emphasizes the significance of the
cause for which this essay is arguing?" and "How does this excerpt leave
readers with a final thought about the piece's claim?" Once students can
answer these questions, which focus on metacognitive awareness of how
argument authors make their works as strong as possible, they're ready
for the next step of the process: applying this writing strategy to their
own works.

4)   Work with Students as They Craft Conclusions to Their Own
      Argument Essays

I recommend asking students to create conclusions to their own argument
essays and then analyze the effectiveness of those conclusions. To conduct
this analysis, students should examine their works and determine how
well they perform the key actions of an argument essay's conclusion:
emphasizing the significance of the essay's cause and leaving readers with
a final thought about the piece's claim. As the students work on their
conclusions, I like to confer with them, asking analytical questions like
"How does your conclusion emphasize the significance of your essay's
cause?" and "What final thought about your essay's claim does your
conclusion leave your reader with?"

I recently spoke with a middle schooler about the conclusion to his
argument essay, focusing on how he felt his work meets the criteria discussed in this chapter. The student asserted that his work, which focuses
on the importance of purchasing and eating local foods, performs the key
actions of a conclusion: "I think I did a good job in my conclusion of
emphasizing the importance of eating local foods because I talk about
how they can be healthier for people and are usually fresher. I also think
I did a good job of leaving readers with a final thought because I talk

about the importance of community as my final thought. I talk about how I think supporting the local community is important and say that people who eat local foods support their local communities." As this student's comments reveal, his conclusion meets the standards of quality for an effective conclusion: it highlights the significance of the essay's cause and leaves readers with an important big-picture idea to consider.

5) Have Students Reflect on Why Their Conclusions Are
Important to Their Own Argument Writing

I recommend concluding this instructional process by asking students to think about why their conclusions are important to their argument essays, as doing so requires students to consider the importance of this writing tool. To facilitate this, I ask students to reflect on the following questions: "Why do you believe it's important that the conclusion to your argument essay highlights the significance of your essay's cause?" and "Why is it important that your conclusion also leaves readers with a final thought about your essay's claim?" The student described in the previous recommendation who wrote an essay arguing in favor of local foods responded to the first question by saying, "I think it's important that my conclusion highlights the significance of my essay's cause because the conclusion gives me a last chance to convince people reading the essay that eating local foods is a really important thing. I definitely need to take advantage of that last chance to make my essay as convincing as it can be."

This student then answered the second question by explaining, "It's important that my conclusion leaves readers with a final thought about the essay's claim because that final thought gives them something they'll really remember. I think people will really remember my final point about supporting local communities because everyone has some kind of community and usually people want to support it. My final point helps people understand that eating local foods supports local communities." This student's responses to these questions show his understanding of how these features maximize the effectiveness of his conclusion. In addition, this insightful understanding suggests that he will continue to incorporate these attributes in his future argument writing conclusions.

Final Thoughts on Creating an Effective Concluding Section

- ◆ Creating an effective concluding section to an argument essay is addressed in Common Core Writing Standards W.6.1.E, W.7.1.E, and W.8.1.E.
- ◆ A strong concluding section to an argument essay should:
  - ◆ Emphasize the significance of the cause for which the essay is arguing.

- ◆ Leave readers with a final thought about the piece's claim.
- ◆ Emphasizing the significance of the cause for which the essay is arguing is important because it helps readers feel that they have read about a topic that is worthy of their time and consideration.
- ◆ Leaving readers with a final thought about the piece's claim is important because it gives readers an idea to continue to consider once they've finished the essay, such as how the essay's topic relates to "big-picture" societal issues. Essays that do this can impact readers and stay in their minds once they've finished the piece.
- ◆ When teaching students about creating an effective concluding section:
  - ◆ Show students examples of strong conclusions to argument essays and discuss the features of those conclusions.
  - ◆ Discuss with students why strong conclusions are important to effective argument writing.
  - ◆ Ask students to analyze why the features of strong conclusions are important.
  - ◆ Work with students as they craft conclusions to their own argument essays.
  - ◆ Have students reflect on why their conclusions are important to their own argument writing.

Section 2

Putting It Together

8

Assessment Strategies

How Should We Assess Students' Argument Essays?

In this chapter, we'll examine specific evaluation criteria and rubrics to use when evaluating your students' argument essays. Each of this book's preceding chapters focuses on a specific attribute, or tool, of effective argument writing; I recommend keeping this same tool-focused mindset when evaluating students' argument essays. To apply the toolkit idea to the assessment of students' argument essays, separately evaluate each attribute of effective argument writing in students' works by using distinct rubrics that represent the standards of quality for each of these writing strategies. These rubrics enable you to provide separate scores and feedback for students' performances on each of these attributes. For example, I recently worked with a student who scored a four (out of four) on five of the attributes of effective argument writing discussed in this book, but earned scores of two for both her introduction and conclusion. These scores showed me that this student had mastered the writing strategies associated with composing the body of an argument essay but needed some additional support in ways to create effective introductions and conclusions. Another middle school student with whom I worked had a very different score breakdown: he scored highly on all of the argument writing attributes described in this book except for supporting claims with reasons and evidence while using credible sources, on which he scored a one. This suggests that he did strong work overall, but needed help finding and using credible sources to support his claims.

Although both of these students did well on their essays, a specific look at their scores shows differences in their areas of strength and areas of need; assigning them with general grades that don't address specific attributes of effective argument writing wouldn't provide this precise information. I like to tell students that I evaluate them on individual attributes of effective argument writing because it "helps me help [them] as much as possible by giving really specific information about what's going well and what can be better." With this specificity in mind, let's take a look at particular evaluation criteria you can use when assessing your students on each of the argument writing tools described in this book.

Introducing Claims

The first argument writing tool discussed in this book is introducing the claim that the author will develop in an argument essay. Table 8.1 lists the evaluation criteria I use when evaluating how well a student has applied this writing strategy to his or her work. (Reproducible versions of all the tables given in this chapter can be found in Appendix B.) The evaluation questions for this component of effective argument writing correspond with the key elements of effectively introduced claims described in Chapter 1: 1) Effectively communicating the issue the rest of the piece will be describing, and 2) Clearly taking a side on an issue. In addition to these evaluation questions, this rubric has space for the teacher to record comments on how each student introduced the claims in his or her piece.

When I use these criteria to evaluate the introductory section of an argument essay, I focus on how well the author identifies the piece's topic and asserts his or her position on that topic. I explain to my students, "I should read your introductory paragraph and have a clear understanding of what issue you'll be explaining to me and how you feel about that issue. This will prepare me for all of the other information you'll give me as I keep reading."

TABLE 8.1 Evaluation Criteria for Introducing Claims

Writing Tool	Evaluation Criteria	Possible Points	Your Score
Introducing claims	◆ Does the introductory paragraph effectively communicate to readers the issue the rest of the piece will be describing? ◆ Does the author clearly communicate his or her position on this issue?	4	

Comments:

Acknowledging Alternate and Opposing Claims

I recommend evaluating how effectively students have acknowledged alternate and opposing claims in their argument essays by considering two ideas: 1) If the piece clearly incorporates a point of view that differs from the author's claim, and 2) If the essay includes information that refutes this claim. When explaining these evaluation criteria to my students, I emphasize the ideas raised in Chapter 2 about why each one is important: including alternate and/or opposing points of view shows that the author has thought about other possibilities and still believes in his or her position, and refuting these points of view gives the author an additional opportunity to assert that his or her position is strongest of all possible stances on the issue. Table 8.2 includes the evaluation questions I use to assess my students' performance in acknowledging alternate and opposing claims.

You may recall the student work depicted in Chapter 2 in which a student arguing in favor of hybrid cars acknowledged and refuted views that opposed this perspective. I explained to this student that he scored highly on this writing strategy because of the way he "clearly states a reasonable point that the opposition might make and then proceeds to refute this point with evidence, making this essay especially strong."

Supporting Claims with Reasons and Evidence while Using Credible Sources

This argument writing tool is significant because a piece that doesn't support its claims using credible sources is unlikely to be as effective as possible in convincing readers to buy into the author's argument. When evaluating a piece on this standard of quality, I focus on the following attributes: 1) If the essay includes reasons and evidence that clearly and

TABLE 8.2 Evaluation Criteria for Acknowledging Alternate and Opposing Claims

Writing Tool	Evaluation Criteria	Possible Points	Your Score
Acknowledging alternate or opposing claims	◆ Does the piece clearly incorporate an alternate or opposing view that differs from the author's claim? ◆ Does the piece include information that refutes this alternate or opposing claim?	4	

Comments:

TABLE 8.3 Evaluation Criteria for Supporting Claims with Reasons and Evidence while Using Credible Sources

Writing Tool	Evaluation Criteria	Possible Points	Your Score
Supporting claims with reasons and evidence while using credible sources	◆ Does the essay include reasons and evidence that clearly and effectively support the author's claim? ◆ Are these reasons and evidence drawn from credible sources?	4	

Comments:

effectively support the author's claim, and 2) If the reasons and evidence are drawn from credible sources. I recently incorporated these standards of quality in a conversation with a middle schooler about her argument essay: the student's essay focused on preserving a local park that it was rumored would be eliminated as part of a construction project. She incorporated a number of reasons and evidence in her essay, but the information she included focused more on the history of parks in the United States than on pieces of evidence closely aligned with preserving this specific park, such as its impact on its local community and the significance of the plants and wildlife living there. Once she found information from credible sources that directly supported her claim and incorporated it into her essay, her piece became much stronger. Table 8.3 gives the rubric I use to evaluate students on this important writing tool.

Organizing Reasons and Evidence Logically

Another key component to effective argument writing is organizing reasons and evidence logically; strong argument essays use paragraphs to group related information together and organize those paragraphs in clear and logical ways that support the piece's main idea. A piece without a strong sense of organization is distracting to readers—for example, if I was reading an argument essay that did not divide separate points into distinct paragraphs, I might focus more on the piece's lack of organization than on its argument. When I evaluate a piece of argument writing for this strategy, I hone in on the following characteristics: 1) If the essay's paragraphs are clearly divided into separate ideas, and 2) If the paragraphs are sequenced in a logical manner, such as an introductory paragraph, others that support the piece's claim, another that describes alternate or opposing claims, and then a concluding paragraph. Table 8.4 contains the evaluation questions I use to assess students' works with this writing tool in mind:

TABLE 8.4 Evaluation Criteria for Organizing Reasons and Evidence Logically

Writing Tool	Evaluation Criteria	Possible Points	Your Score
Organizing reasons and evidence logically	◆ Are the essay's paragraphs clearly divided into separate ideas? ◆ Are the paragraphs sequenced in a logical way, such as beginning with an introduction, moving to paragraphs that support the piece's claim, transitioning to discussions of alternate or opposing claims, and then finishing with a concluding section?	4	

Comments:

A middle school student with whom I recently conferenced did a very good job of explaining to me how she organized reasons and evidence logically in her argument essay on the benefits of children having pets: "I made sure to separate all of my different ideas into paragraphs," she explained. "Sometimes, when writing essays when I was younger, I would separate the essay into paragraphs but not really pay attention to whether the paragraphs had different ideas in them. I paid attention to this when writing this essay, and I think it made the organization of this essay so much better." This student's comments reveal her understanding of the importance of this writing strategy as well her awareness of specific ways she applied it to her own writing.

Using Words, Phrases, and Clauses to Create Cohesion and Clarify Relationships

A strong argument essay uses words, phrases, and clauses to create cohesion and clarify relationships between statements. For example, an effective argument author will connect related statements with phrases such as "in addition" and "for example," and will use language such as "however" and "despite this" to signal distinctions between pieces of information. When evaluating student work with this writing tool in mind, I focus on the following criteria: 1) If the piece contains words, phrases, and clauses that create cohesion and clarify relationships between both similar

TABLE 8.5 Evaluation Criteria for Using Words, Phrases, and Clauses to Create Cohesion and Clarify Relationships

Writing Tool	Evaluation Criteria	Possible Points	Your Score
Using words, phrases, and clauses to create cohesion and clarify relationships	◆ Does the piece contain words, phrases, and clauses that create cohesion and clarify relationships between both similar and dissimilar ideas? ◆ Are these words, phrases, and clauses used effectively and accurately?	4	

Comments:

and dissimilar ideas, 2) If these words, phrases, and clauses are used effectively and accurately. Table 8.5 lists the evaluation criteria I use to assess how well students have used words, phrases, and clauses to create cohesion and clarify relationships.

I use these standards of quality to ensure that students not only use language that creates cohesion and clarifies relationships, but also that they use these words, phrases, and clauses in ways that make sense. For example, I once conferred with a student who confused the meaning of some of the words, phrases, and clauses that clarify relationships; at times, he used phrases that communicate similarities between ideas (like "in addition") when he meant to use language that indicates differences (such as "in contrast"). Once this student revised his work so that his words, phrases, and clauses accurately indicated the relationships between ideas in his essay, his work became much stronger and easier to understand.

Establishing and Maintaining a Formal Style

Another important aspect of effective argument writing is establishing and maintaining a formal style, which enables argument essays to align with the expectations of argument writing. Formal language allows argument authors to appeal to the widest audience possible and maximizes their chances of being taken seriously by that audience. When evaluating a piece of argument writing for this attribute, I consider the following criteria: 1) If the essay clearly uses formal language designed to appeal to a wide audience and ensure the piece's claims will be taken seriously by that audience, and 2) If the essay uses this language form consistently throughout the piece. I assess students' performances on these criteria using the rubric given in Table 8.6.

TABLE 8.6 Evaluation Criteria for Establishing and Maintaining a Formal Style

Writing Tool	Evaluation Criteria	Possible Points	Your Score
Establishing and maintaining a formal style	◆ Does the essay clearly use formal language designed to appeal to a wide audience and ensure the piece's claims will be taken seriously by that audience? ◆ Does the essay use formal language consistently throughout the piece?	4	

Comments:

A middle school student with whom I spoke about this topic did an excellent job of explaining how she applied these criteria to her essay: "I wrote about how I think it's important that all kids participate in sports because of all the different ways sports can help them, like learning team-work and being in shape. I used formal language the whole time I was writing the essay." She continued on to say, "There were times when I almost used informal language, like the kind of slang I'd use with my friends, but I caught myself and used formal language because formal language allows more people to understand what I'm saying and helps them take it seriously." This student's comments not only reveal her understanding of how she used this writing tool, but also indicate an excellent awareness of its benefits.

Creating an Effective Concluding Section

When evaluating the effectiveness of students' concluding sections, I focus on the following criteria: 1) If the conclusion emphasizes the significance of the cause for which the essay is arguing, and 2) If that conclusion leaves readers with a final thought about the piece's claim. The first of these criteria identifies reasons that the piece's topic is important, while the second provides a "big-picture" idea that connects the essay's argument with a larger societal issue. Conclusions that score highly on these criteria go beyond basic summaries of the piece's claim and help keep readers engaged through the end of the essay. Table 8.7 gives a rubric I use to evaluate students' conclusions.

I recently spoke with a middle school student who told me that these criteria were useful to him as he worked to create an effective conclusion. "I never really knew what made a conclusion good," this student told me.

TABLE 8.7 Evaluation Criteria for Creating an Effective Concluding Section

Writing Tool	Evaluation Criteria	Possible Points	Your Score
Creating an effective concluding section	◆ Does the conclusion emphasize the significance of the cause for which the essay is arguing? ◆ Does the conclusion leave readers with a final thought about the piece's claim?	4	

Comments:

"I just knew I was supposed to write them. Now I think my conclusions are much better because I know what makes a conclusion really good."

A Note on Using These Evaluation Criteria

This approach to assessing argument writing is designed to evaluate students on distinct writing tools, but it's important to note that you don't have to always evaluate students on all seven tools at once. I like to begin a unit on argument writing by assessing students' works on two fundamental writing tools, such as introducing claims and using reasons and evidence from credible sources to support those claims. Once it seems like students have mastered these concepts, I introduce new, slightly more nuanced tools, such as organizing reasons and evidence logically and using language that creates cohesion and clarifies relationships. Evaluating students on specific writing tools also presents opportunities for differentiation: while some students might complete an argument essay and be ready to be evaluated on all seven of the tools described in this chapter, others might be best served by being evaluated on four or five at that particular time and being evaluated on the others later in the school year when they've had more time to develop as writers. I encourage you to take advantage of the flexibility inherent in these writing tools to make your argument writing assessment as meaningful and helpful for your students as possible.

Final Thoughts on Assessing Students' Argument Writing

◆ I recommend separately evaluating each attribute of effective argument writing in students' works by doing the following:
  ◆ Giving students rubrics that represent the standards of quality for individual writing strategies.

- ◆ Providing separate scores and feedback for each student's performance on these distinct attributes.
- ◆ Each of the writing tools discussed in this book represents an attribute on which students' argument essays can be evaluated.
- ◆ Evaluating students on specific attributes provides clear feedback on which writing tools they have mastered and which remain areas of need.
- ◆ You don't need to evaluate students on all seven argument writing tools at one time. I recommend beginning by assessing students' works on two fundamental concepts and then adding more complex ones over time.

9

Final Thoughts and Tips for Classroom Practice

How Can We Put the Ideas in this Book into Practice?

In the introductory chapter of this book, we met Kate, a first-year middle school teacher needing support and resources to help her students with argument writing. Kate acknowledged the importance of argument writing, but struggled with explaining the features of strong argument essays to her students. Kate's problem can be solved with the toolkit approach that is central to this book: when students read effective argument essays and analyze the attributes (or tools) that make those essays effective, they can then apply those same writing tools to their own argument pieces. This instructional approach, which focuses on students' awareness and application of the components of strong argument writing, is especially important given the challenges this genre poses for many middle school teachers (Moss, 2014) and the Common Core State Standards' statement that argument writing is important to college- and career-readiness.

In this chapter, we'll examine six key recommendations for putting the ideas discussed in this book into action with your students:

- ◆ Show students examples of specific writing tools in quality argument essays.
- ◆ Talk with students about why each one of these writing tools is important to effective argument writing.
- ◆ Have students work on activities in which they analyze the importance of specific argument writing tools.
- ◆ Ask students to apply each of the argument writing tools to their own works.

- Help students reflect on the importance of each of the argument writing tools to their own argument writing.
- Evaluate students on their uses of specific argument writing tools.

These recommendations combine to create an instructional process that helps students read argument essays "as writers." In other words, students who follow these suggestions will not just read argument essays to comprehend the text, but also to learn the strategies used by other argument authors and apply them to their own pieces. Now, let's look at these suggestions in detail.

Recommendation One: Show Students Examples of Specific Writing Tools in Quality Argument Essays

The first step in helping students understand and use specific argument writing strategies is to show them examples (also known as mentor texts) of how these strategies are used in quality argument essays. I tell students that looking at examples of argument writing tools in the context of argument essays allows them to see these writing strategies in their "natural habitats": the authentic ways they are used by writers. Creating a strong argument essay can be challenging, and students need to see quality examples that clearly and effectively use the tactics of high-quality argument essays. When putting this recommendation into action in your classroom, make use of the many resources included in this book, such as Appendix A, which features complete versions of the argument essays presented throughout the book, and the annotated bibliography, which identifies specific excerpts from the essays included in Appendix A that are discussed in the book's chapters and connects each excerpt with a Common Core Writing Standard. When showing your students these examples, clearly identify the strategy you want them to examine. For example, if you want your students to primarily focus on how an essay uses words, phrases, and clauses to create cohesion and clarify relationships, articulate this strategy as the lesson's focus so that students will know to focus on this tool as they read. Once students have seen examples of specific argument writing tools in action, they'll be well-prepared for the next step of this process.

Recommendation Two: Talk with Students about Why Each One of These Writing Tools Is Important to Effective Argument Writing

This instructional recommendation builds on the first suggestion: now that students have read argument essays that contain specific writing tools, they're ready to discuss why these tools are important to effective argument writing. These conversations help students think critically and metacognitively about the significance of particular writing strategies, increasing their awareness of how each strategy enhances a piece of argument writing in a specific way. When holding these discussions with your students, I recommend comparing an argument essay that uses a particular strategy with a version of that essay that doesn't use that strategy; this helps students clearly understand the importance of that writing tool to the original version. For example, when talking with your students about the importance of introducing claims to effective argument writing, show them an introductory paragraph from an argument essay that introduces its piece's claim and juxtapose it with a revised version of that paragraph that doesn't contain the original claim-introducing language. Once you've done this, talk with your students about why the claim-introducing language is important to the original version, focusing on why this is an important component of an effective argument essay. No matter which argument writing tool you're discussing with your students, showing them examples of argument writing with and without that tool can facilitate a discussion of the significance of that concept to creating a strong argument essay.

Recommendation Three: Have Students Work on Activities in Which They Analyze the Importance of Specific Argument Writing Tools

Asking students to work individually or in small groups on activities in which they analyze the importance of specific argument tools gives them even more responsibility for their learning. These activities make this instructional process more hands-on for students and allow them to apply the ideas and analysis they began to learn in the second instructional recommendation to other examples of argument writing. The specific activities in which you'll engage your students will vary somewhat with different argument writing tools, but all of the activities related to this instructional recommendation should ask your students to examine pieces of argument writing and consider why a particular writing strategy can make that piece as effective as possible.

Let's examine some different ways these activities can take shape in your classroom. When focusing on the concept of using words, phrases, and clauses to create cohesion and clarify relationships, I suggest giving students argument essays that utilize this writing tool, asking them to identify the language that creates cohesion and clarifies relationships, and then having them rewrite the passage without this language. After doing so, the students can analyze why these words, phrases, and clauses are important to the original text. When working on the writing strategy of establishing and maintaining a formal style, I recommend giving students argument essays written in formal language, instructing them to "translate" them into informal language, and then asking them to consider the significance of formal language to the effectiveness of the original essay. While the specific activities in these examples vary somewhat based on each one's focal strategy, both examples give students ownership over their learning by asking them to change an aspect of an argument writing essay and analyze why that aspect is important to the success of the original piece.

Recommendation Four: Ask Students to Apply Each of the Argument Writing Tools to Their Own Works

Once students have thoughtfully analyzed the significance of specific writing tools to effective argument essays, the next step is to give them even more responsibility by asking them to apply these writing strategies to their own works. Doing so gets students even more actively involved in their learning, as it enables them to use these writing tools to enhance their own essays. When engaging your students in this activity, I recommend briefly reviewing some examples of the concept you've been studying and then telling the students they're ready to apply that writing tool to their own argument essays. As students write, I suggest conferring with them individually and checking in on how well each student is understanding and using the focal strategy. In these one-on-one meetings, you can provide students with reinforcement and instruction suited to their needs, such as checking to see if they used the concept correctly and clarifying any confusion they have about how to integrate it into their works.

Recommendation Five: Help Students Reflect on the Importance of Each of the Argument Writing Tools to Their Own Argument Writing

I recommend following up on the students' application of a specific writing strategy to their essays by asking them to reflect on the benefits of using this strategy. For example, if students have just finished applying the writing tool of acknowledging alternate and opposing claims to their argument essays, I'll ask them to reflect on the following questions: "Why is it important that your argument essay acknowledges alternate or opposing claims?" and "How would your essay be different if it didn't acknowledge these claims?" These questions require students to go beyond simply using this strategy in their works, requiring them to also consider why this strategy is important to their essays and how the essay would differ without the application of this strategy. I tell my students that I want them to understand *why* certain pieces of writing are effective; reflection questions such as these help students reach this understanding.

Recommendation Six: Evaluate Students on Their Uses of Specific Argument Writing Tools

Finally, I recommend evaluating students on their uses of specific argument writing tools to clearly communicate how well a student has mastered a specific strategy that is important to effective argument writing. The rubrics and criteria discussed in Chapter 8 will help you assess students' performances in applying the writing tools discussed in this book to their own argument essays and allow you to express students' abilities to use these strategies. The clear communication these rubrics provide about students' mastery of distinct argument writing tools helps them understand which strategies students are using effectively in their works and the ones with which they need additional support. In their book, *Evaluating Children's Writing*, Suzanne Bratcher and Linda Ryan (2004) define grading as "communication between teacher and student designed to enhance the student's writing" (p. 9); the use of individual, strategy-focused rubrics that express how well students have mastered specific writing tools can provide the kind of effective communication that Bratcher and Ryan describe.

Final Thoughts on the Argument Writing Toolkit

I recently led a conference session on argument writing instruction, which the teachers and administrators attending the conference identified as a challenging and important topic. While I still remember many of the questions audience members asked me, the one that stood out the most was: "What's more important—reading argument essays or writing them?" This question stayed with me because of its relation to what research reveals about effective writing instruction and to the message that I present in this book: reading and writing are equally important to our students' writing development because the texts our students read can increase their knowledge of how to write well (Ray, 1999). As Kelly Gallagher (2014) explains, "Before our students can write well in a given discourse, they need to see good writing in that discourse" (p. 28). When our students identify, analyze, implement, and finally reflect on specific argument writing strategies, they are linking reading and writing in ways that can't be undone. As you put the ideas in this book into practice in your classroom, emphasize the connection between students' reading and analyzing effective argument writing and putting the tools that make those pieces successful into action in their own works. If anyone ever asks you if reading or writing argument essays is more important, you can respond as I did at that conference: "Students begin to learn the tools of argument writing when they read; they then practice with those tools when they write."

Section **3**

Resources

Appendix A
Argument Essays Featured in This Book

Appendix A contains complete versions of the argument essays featured in this book. These essays are mentor texts I wrote to show my middle school students the tools of effective argument writing. I encourage you to use these essays in conjunction with the suggestions and activities described in this book to help your students master the tools of argument writing!

Don't Trust Amazon.com's Customer Reviews

What do you most enjoy about the internet? Some people like the way the internet gives everyone a voice—anyone with internet access can express his or her opinion about anything. There are many ways people can share their opinions online: they can create their own websites and express their thoughts on social networking sites like Facebook and Twitter. In addition, people can share their thoughts by posting product reviews on websites like Amazon.com that sell these items. Amazon.com sells a wide range of objects, and the majority of items for sale on this website have been reviewed by someone. Reviewers rate items by giving between one and five stars and can write a description of their thoughts on the item to go along with this rating. Prospective buyers should not trust these online reviews when making their purchases. Instead, consumers should rely on expert opinions and credible sources when making purchases.

Online reviews may be written by very biased sources. A 2013 *New York Times* article described an investigation by New York law-enforcement agents of companies that create fake online reviews and businesses that hire these companies to do so (Streitfeld, 2013). This article, titled "Giving yourself 5 Stars? Online, it might cost you," explains that some businesses have been paying so-called "reputation" companies to write positive online reviews of their products—regardless of whether or not these reviews are accurate. The article quotes Eric Schneidermann, the New York Attorney General, who argues that fake online reviews are especially dishonest: "When you look at a billboard, you can tell it's a paid advertisement—but on Yelp or Citysearch, you assume you're reading authentic consumer opinions, making this practice even more deceiving." Fake online reviews have become so problematic and widespread that researchers from Cornell University have developed a computer program designed to detect dishonest reviews (Ott, Choi, Cardie, & Hancock, 2011). The combination of the New York investigation and the need for the

Cornell computer program strongly suggests that online reviews have the strong possibility of being untrustworthy.

Some people say that online reviews should be trusted because of the way they allow all people an opportunity to share their thoughts. People who hold this belief might feel that it is useful to read comments from anyone who wants to review an item, regardless of that person's qualifications. Despite these widespread beliefs, this availability to the general public is precisely the problem with online reviews; when all people can review items, there is no guarantee that the reviewers will be knowledgeable about a product and present an unbiased opinion.

If you want to know the most accurate and unbiased information about products you're interested in purchasing, pay attention to unbiased expert reviews published in reputable newspapers and magazines. Untrustworthy reviews on websites like Amazon.com have become a major problem for consumers, who can no longer be sure if they are reading the opinion of another honest customer or someone hired by a company to make a product look good and increase its sales. The problem of potentially dishonest internet reviews is a new issue in our society; before the widespread use of online communication, we did not have so many places to find out information. Now that we do, we must be very careful about what sources we trust.

Keep Gym Class in Schools

The people in charge of our schools make a lot of tough decisions. Politicians, school board members, and policy makers have to think about issues like what books should be taught, whether or not schools should have dress codes, and how much time students should spend on different activities. Deciding how much time students should spend on different activities can be especially difficult. With new, challenging standards like the Common Core State Standards being used in schools and limited amounts of money, some schools have cut or reduced "specials" like gym class. These administrators should keep gym class in schools. Gym is a valuable part of the school experience that increases students' chances to live happy, successful lives and should not be eliminated.

One of the many ways gym classes benefit students is that, according to recent research, students who are physically fit perform better academically. A study published in *The Journal of Pediatrics* examined the aerobic fitness and reading and math test scores of almost 12,000 elementary and middle school students in Nebraska; the researchers found that aerobically fit students were more likely than aerobically unfit students to pass the state's reading and math tests. According to the study's authors, "to improve academic performance, schools should focus on the aerobic fitness of every student" (Rauner, Walters, Avery, & Wanser, 2013, p. 344).

This study's results clearly reveal a benefit of gym classes: fit students are more likely to succeed academically.

Some may say that devoting time and money to gym classes detracts from what many believe is the essential mission of schools: educating students in academic subjects and teaching them as much as possible. However, as the aforementioned study from *The Journal of Pediatrics* explains, students' fitness levels are important indicators of their academic performances. In addition, childhood obesity is a major public health issue in the United States; the Centers for Disease Control state that obesity among adolescents has more than quadrupled in the past 30 years and assert that obese children and adolescents have high risks of serious health problems as adults, such as heart disease and several types of cancer (Centers for Disease Control, 2014). Schools that emphasize physical activity can be part of the solution to this major health problem facing America's youth.

Gym class is an important part of the school curriculum that, according to research, helps maximize student success. In today's high-stakes-testing environment and increasingly innovative world, our students need as much support as possible. Keeping gym class in school is an opportunity to help students achieve high academic goals while also contributing to the health of our country's youth. These academic and health benefits can positively impact our society in a number of ways, ranging from more students attending college to fewer health problems among children. So, if anyone ever asks if you believe gym class is important, say "Yes! It keeps our young people fit and intelligent—a great combination!"

Lower the Cost of College

Each year, millions of young people enroll in America's colleges. Excited by the opportunities of college and optimistic about their futures, these students frequently see college as a step toward realizing their dreams. Some may dream of being teachers, others might hope to be doctors, and some might even think about being the President of the United States. College is often thought of as a time to explore new ideas by taking interesting classes, joining exciting groups, and making new friends. However, the high price of college is impacting many students' futures: the money that students need to borrow in order to attend college is limiting their opportunities after it. College needs to cost less in order to help more young people achieve their goals.

The high costs of college are making it difficult for young college graduates to live independently. An educational research organization called The Institute for College Access and Success (TICAS) explains that two-thirds of American college graduates graduate in debt from student loans, and the average borrower will owe $26,600 in these loans

(TICAS, 2013). One effect of these student loans is that more recent college graduates are living with their parents than ever before (Weissman, 2013). In an article in *The Atlantic* magazine, author Jordan Weissman explains that "61 percent more college-educated 18–34-year-olds were living with their families in 2011 than in 2001." Lauren Asher, the president of TICAS, says in an article in *Forbes* magazine that the increased student debt faced by recent graduates results in them needing to delay their independence: "Debt costs you time in savings, pushes back when and whether you can buy a home, start a family, open a small business or access capital" (Denhart, 2013).

Some people oppose efforts to decrease college costs, asserting that making colleges cheaper for students will require the government to spend money to offset the lower tuition amounts that the colleges receive and that the government cannot afford to do so. While the government may need to spend money for college costs to decrease, there are a number of ways that having a highly educated and debt-free population can positively impact society. Young people in a great deal of debt can't purchase many things, which hurts the economy. If recent college graduates are concerned with paying off their loans and not purchasing houses and cars, the housing and auto industries may decline. However, these and other businesses may thrive if young people are not overcome with debt. Also, a country with more well-educated people contains more individuals who can produce innovations, ideas, and products that can bring profit to the country's industries and create jobs. If the government invests in helping students graduate debt-free from college, these promising possibilities may become reality.

Lowering the cost of college will significantly increase the opportunities available to recent graduates; people who graduate college without a great deal of debt can make significant purchases and achieve independence at younger ages than those who owe tens or hundreds of thousands of dollars upon graduation. In addition, issues related to student debt impact the ability to improve one's life that many people call the American Dream, which has long been considered central to America's identity as a land of opportunity. The extreme amount of debt facing many young people today makes it much more challenging for them to lead successful and productive lives. Reducing the cost of college—and the student debt that accompanies it—makes the American Dream increasingly possible.

The Importance of Baseball

A frequent conversation topic among sports fans is the relevance of baseball. While many people are fans of the game, there are others who insist that it has been overtaken by other, faster-paced sports such as football, basketball, and automobile racing. While it is true that these sports are much more popular today than they were 50 years ago, their increased popularity does not mean baseball is any less significant. Although society has changed in many ways since its origins in the 1800s, baseball remains an extremely important sport in America and around the world.

One indicator of baseball's importance is its global popularity. Although it has been traditionally called America's "National Pastime," baseball has been embraced by athletes in countries around the world. One example of this is the World Baseball Classic, a tournament in which countries from all over the globe compete. The World Baseball Classic has grown so much in popularity around the world that event organizers increased the amount of competing countries from 16 in 2009 to 28 in 2013 (MLB, 2011). In addition, games of the 2013 World Baseball Classic were played in four different countries: Japan, Puerto Rico, Taiwan, and the United States of America (Sports Illustrated for Kids, 2013). The World Baseball Classic is a key representation of baseball's global appeal.

Baseball's importance also lies in how closely its major events are intertwined with key events in American history. Ken Burns' (1994) PBS documentary film, *Baseball*, asserts that baseball is a lens through which to view the major movements in American history. Burns' film explains that key issues in America's past such as immigration, segregation, and the rise of mass communication are all reflected in the history of baseball. For example, Burns describes how baseball played a key role in the lives of immigrants to America in the early 20th century: the game provided an opportunity for immigrants to immerse themselves in the American culture and helped ease their transition to their new country.

Some detractors of baseball say that the game only remains popular and important among specific segments of the population, such as older people who enjoy a slower-paced sport or individuals in particular places where the game is disproportionately popular. Still others contend that baseball's time has simply passed. These individuals may say that, while the sport was once thought of as our nation's pastime, it is no longer very popular or relevant, because it doesn't deliver a great deal of high-speed action like football, basketball, and automobile racing do. They might claim that we live in an age when people want high-speed, action-packed entertainment, and baseball is not relevant in a society that values these characteristics. Despite these beliefs that some hold, baseball has attracted many fans in recent years: the last decade has produced all ten of the best-attended Major League Baseball seasons in history and the average major league baseball game in 2014 averaged over 30,000 fans in attendance (MLB, 2014a). In addition, baseball's connection to American culture and history speaks to its continued relevance, since major figures in baseball history such as Jackie Robinson and Hank Aaron are connected to important cultural events in American history.

Baseball's importance and relevance in the 21st century is multi-layered. It is now a sport that is popular all over the world, as evidenced by the World Baseball Classic and the increasing amount of international players on Major League rosters—over 25 percent of the players on Major League teams at the beginning of the 2014 season were born outside the United States (MLB, 2014b). Baseball also retains its popularity in America, as the previously mentioned attendance figures and connections to American culture indicate. So, if anyone ever suggests to you that baseball is losing its importance, explain that this is far from the truth: 21st century baseball is a combination of global diversity and American history that is unrivaled by any other sport.

Introverts Can Be Great Leaders, Too

Picture a leader in your mind; what do you envision? Do you think of a person with a booming voice and the "in your face" style frequently associated with football coaches and military officers? While many people associate the word "leader" with an outgoing, gregarious nature and extroverted personality, this perception doesn't always align with reality: leadership isn't specific to a particular disposition or persona. Introverted people can be great leaders, just as extroverts can.

Many effective leaders throughout history have been introverts. Jennifer Kahnweiler, in her 2009 book *The Introverted Leader*, identifies famous executives and leaders such as Bill Gates, Mother Theresa, and Abraham Lincoln as naturally introverted. In many ways, explains Kahnweiler, these leaders may have actually been helped by being introverted, as introverts are especially good at thinking and processing their ideas before acting. The introverted nature of these people shows that introverts have held leadership roles for a long time and suggests that they will continue to do so in the future.

Not only can introverts and extroverts both be effective leaders, but research published in 2010 in the *Harvard Business Review* explains that, when employees of a company are proactive and offer ideas to improve the company, introverted leaders are more effective than extroverted ones (Grant, Gino, & Hofman, 2010). The introverted leaders described in the study "listened carefully and made employees feel valued, motivating them to work hard." The authors of this study explain that "it's worth reexamining that stereotype" that effective leaders are always extroverts, as there are many situations where this is not the case.

Some may claim that outgoing and extroverted people are best suited to leadership because extroverts can use their verbal skills to inspire others. However, a leader can inspire others in a variety of ways, not just through oral language. Leaders' actions and achievements can be just as inspirational as motivational speeches. Other people feel that introverts and extroverts can both be leaders in some situations, but specific situations call for extroverted leaders. Despite this belief that some hold, just as there are a variety of ways to inspire others, there are a variety of ways to lead in all situations. While some situations might be most commonly associated with vocal leaders, that doesn't mean introverts can't be equally successful in them. Successful sports coaches have a range of personalities and styles, from vocal to quiet, contemplative personas. Similarly, research on effective teachers shows that individuals with a wide range of personalities can become strong teachers that successfully engage and lead their students through learning activities (Wiens & Ruday, 2014).

Schools, employers, community organizations, and others charged with appointing individuals to leadership positions should take into account the varied personalities that effective leaders can have. Those who dismiss the idea that both introverts and extroverts can be effective leaders may overlook very talented people. It would be very unfortunate if leaders such as Bill Gates, Mother Theresa, and Abraham Lincoln were not given opportunities because of their introverted natures. The idea that individuals with a range of personalities can effectively lead also speaks to an overarching societal issue: common perceptions of who should hold certain roles can be very limiting. We should reconsider assumptions and be aware of different ways people can display abilities and perform tasks effectively.

Schools Should Stay Away from Computer Grading

How are computers used in your school? They might be used by students for typing papers, creating presentations, and doing research. They might be used by teachers for taking attendance, recording students' grades, and emailing administrators. A hot topic in education today is the idea that computer programs can grade students' writing. Software developers have recently created programs that can grade students' papers, creating a situation in which teachers no longer grade their students' works. These programs have been adopted in several colleges and even some middle and high schools. Even though computer programs that grade student writing are gaining popularity, schools should stay away from them. Computer grading does not provide students with important benefits that teacher grading does.

A careful look at the evidence about computer grading shows that grading programs are not very reliable methods of evaluating student writing. According to a news report by Molly Bloom of NPR, Les Perelman, director of the writing center at MIT, experimented with a computer grading program and found a number of inaccuracies (Bloom, 2012). For example, when Perelman wrote a sample essay that was graded by a computer grading program, he noted that the program identified some sections of the essay as incorrect that were actually correct and didn't notice some punctuation mistakes that Perelman intentionally included. Perelman summarized the accuracy of the computer grading program by explaining, "In other words, it doesn't work very well."

Some proponents of computer grading point out the way it gives students faster evaluations than hand-graded essays and contend that this immediate feedback would benefit students. For example, Anant Agarwal, the president of an organization called edX that offers courses online, is quoted in a *New York Times* article on this topic as saying, "There is a huge value in learning with instant feedback" (Markoff, 2013). However, despite any benefits associated with immediate feedback, the problems with computer grading are more significant, such as Les Perelman's previously mentioned research findings on the inaccuracies of computer grading programs. Another problem that outweighs the benefits of computer grading relates to the knowledge that teachers have of their students and those students' abilities. Writing-instruction experts Ralph Fletcher and Joann Portalupi explain that a key component of providing useful feedback to student writers is the teacher's understanding of that student. A computer grading program cannot possess this same type of awareness.

Computer grading has become a popular trend in some circles, but research studies and expert opinions on writing assessment strongly advise against it. Since today's schools value rigorous standards and assessments, it is especially important that students receive accurate, high-quality feedback from teachers who know them well and are familiar with their works—features that are best provided by human grading. The conflict between human vs. computer grading raises an intriguing question with great relevance to life today—Is it better to choose a new technique because it is faster and technology-based, or is it better to choose a technique that isn't as fast but is significantly more effective? Computer grading is appealing to some because it is faster and tech-oriented, but it certainly is not the best choice for our schools and students.

Smaller Classes, Successful Students

Walk into a classroom in a public school, and you are likely to see dedicated teachers and hard-working students. However, you are also likely to see more students crammed into each classroom than ever before. The large amount of students in each classroom is an important issue in 21st century schools: according to a 2011 *New York Times* article titled "Tight Budgets Mean Squeeze in Classrooms," funding cuts and teacher layoffs have led to increasingly more students in public school classes (Dillon, 2011). For example, this article states that a proposal in Detroit would increase high school classes to 60 students. It is imperative that schools reverse this trend and ensure small classes for their students. Small classes can maximize their students' chances of success.

Research suggests that teaching students in small classes can maximize students' chances of being successful later in life. For example, a study published in Columbia University's *Teachers College Record* in 2001 called "The Enduring Effects of Small Classes" states that students who are in small classes in early grades are more likely than students in larger classes to get higher grades, score better on standardized tests, graduate from high school, and go to college (Finn, Gerber, Achilles, & Boyd-Zaharias, 2001). The findings of this study make a compelling case for keeping class sizes small, as the increased chances of these long-term successes are important for not only our students but society as a whole.

In addition, smaller class sizes can reduce the number of teachers leaving their profession. The National Commission on Teaching and America's Future reported in 2007 that close to 50 percent of new teachers leave teaching within five years, and a 2002 New York City Department of Education report stated that excessive class size was a major reason teachers left their jobs after only one year (Gallagher, 2002). If schools can maintain smaller class sizes, they can eliminate this significant reason for teachers leaving their jobs, providing schools with continuity and reducing the constant need for schools to train and develop novice teachers.

There are those who believe that schools should not prioritize keeping class sizes small. Those people might say that schools are very expensive to operate and that having more students in a class allows the school to save money and avoid further cutting budgets. According to these people, schools could then use the money they save to pay for things like books, technology, sports equipment, and other items that can enhance students' school experiences. Others say that having more students in a class doesn't necessarily impact how much students learn in a particular class. However, the previously mentioned research suggests the importance of small classes. Small class sizes are not the only factor in students succeeding in school, but they do have important impacts on students' academic careers (as the study "The Enduring Effects of Small Classes" explains).

Instituting small class sizes in today's schools is no easy task: there are many logistical and financial challenges that potentially stand in the way of this goal. However, reducing the number of students in classrooms can significantly improve the lives of young people, as research indicates that small class sizes correlate with students reaching important educational milestones later in life. In addition, small class sizes can play an important role in teacher retention, further strengthening the schools America's children attend. An important issue in our nation's schools is providing a high-quality education for all children, no matter their background or socioeconomic status. While there are many factors that can contribute to a strong educational experience, the issue of small classes is a significant one: small classes can help all students, regardless of background, by maximizing their chances for success and contributing to feelings of continuity and community in their schools.

Appendix B
Reproducible Charts and
Forms You Can Use in Your Classroom

This appendix contains reproducible versions of key charts and forms featured in this book. It is designed to help you put the ideas in this book into action in your classroom!

Figure 2.1 Group Analysis Guideline Sheet

Group Analysis Guideline Sheet:
Acknowledging Alternate and Opposing Claims

Essay title:

Summary of argument:

Text that introduces alternate or opposing claims:

Why you believe it is important that the author acknowledges these alternate or opposing claims:

TABLE 5.1 Text Comparison Template

Original Text	Text with Word, Phrase, or Clause that Creates Cohesion and Clarifies Relationships Removed	Why the Word, Phrase, or Clause that Creates Cohesion and Clarifies Relationships is Important

TABLE 6.1 Formal and Informal Language Template

Original Formal Version	Revised Informal Version	Why the Formal Language Is Important to the Original Passage

TABLE 7.1 Key Actions of an Argument Essay's Conclusion Template

Key Actions	Excerpt from an Argument Essay's Conclusion that Performs These Actions
1. Emphasize the significance of the cause for which the essay is arguing	
2. Leave readers with a final thought about the piece's claim	

TABLE 8.1 Evaluation Criteria for Introducing Claims

Writing Tool	Evaluation Criteria	Possible Points	Your Score
Introducing claims	◆ Does the introductory paragraph effectively communicate to readers the issue the rest of the piece will be describing? ◆ Does the author clearly communicate his or her position on this issue?	4	

Comments:

© 2016, *The Argument Writing Toolkit: Using Mentor Texts in Grades 6–8*, Sean Ruday, Taylor & Francis

TABLE 8.2 Evaluation Criteria for Acknowledging Alternate and Opposing Claims

Writing Tool	Evaluation Criteria	Possible Points	Your Score
Acknowledging alternate or opposing claims	◆ Does the piece clearly incorporate an alternate or opposing view that differs from the author's claim? ◆ Does the piece include information that refutes this alternate or opposing claim?	4	

Comments:

© 2016, *The Argument Writing Toolkit: Using Mentor Texts in Grades 6–8*, Sean Ruday, Taylor & Francis

TABLE 8.3 Evaluation Criteria for Supporting Claims with Reasons and Evidence while Using Credible Sources

Writing Tool	Evaluation Criteria	Possible Points	Your Score
Supporting claims with reasons and evidence while using credible sources	◆ Does the essay include reasons and evidence that clearly and effectively support the author's claim? ◆ Are these reasons and evidence drawn from credible sources?	4	

Comments:

TABLE 8.4 Evaluation Criteria for Organizing Reasons and Evidence Logically

Writing Tool	Evaluation Criteria	Possible Points	Your Score
Organizing reasons and evidence logically	◆ Are the essay's paragraphs clearly divided into separate ideas? ◆ Are the paragraphs sequenced in a logical way, such as beginning with an introduction, moving to paragraphs that support the piece's claim, transitioning to discussions of alternate or opposing claims, and then finishing with a concluding section?	4	

Comments:

TABLE 8.5 Evaluation Criteria for Using Words, Phrases, and Clauses to Create Cohesion and Clarify Relationships

Writing Tool	Evaluation Criteria	Possible Points	Your Score
Using words, phrases, and clauses to create cohesion and clarify relationships	◆ Does the piece contain words, phrases, and clauses that create cohesion and clarify relationships between both similar and dissimilar ideas? ◆ Are these words, phrases, and clauses used effectively and accurately?	4	

Comments:

TABLE 8.6 Evaluation Criteria for Establishing and Maintaining a Formal Style

Writing Tool	Evaluation Criteria	Possible Points	Your Score
Establishing and maintaining a formal style	◆ Does the essay clearly use formal language designed to appeal to a wide audience and ensure the piece's claims will be taken seriously by that audience? ◆ Does the essay use formal language consistently throughout the piece?	4	

Comments:

TABLE 8.7 Evaluation Criteria for Creating an Effective Concluding Section

Writing Tool	Evaluation Criteria	Possible Points	Your Score
Creating an effective concluding section	◆ Does the conclusion emphasize the significance of the cause for which the essay is arguing? ◆ Does the conclusion leave readers with a final thought about the piece's claim?	4	

Comments:

TABLE A.C.1 Graphic Organizer for Selecting a Topic

What Is an Issue about Which You Feel Strongly?	Why Do You Feel Strongly about That Issue?	What Argument Would You Make about This Issue?	What Are Some Highlights from the Evidence You Found Related to This Issue?	Based on This Evidence, What Claim Will You Make in Your Argument Essay?

Appendix C
Thoughts on Selecting Argument Writing Topics

Another important part of teaching students to write argument essays is helping them select topics that are relevant and engaging for them and that are conducive to crafting effective arguments. When I help middle school students think of argument writing topics, I pose the following questions to them:

- What is an issue about which you feel strongly?
- Why do you feel strongly about that issue?
- What argument would you make about this issue?

These questions help students brainstorm issues that matter to them, reflect on why they see these issues as meaningful, and contemplate what arguments they would pose about those issues. Once students have thought about these questions, I ask them to research their topics of interest. I explain to students that, as they find evidence, they will likely need to adjust their claims to align with these pieces of evidence; as George Hillocks (2010) states, the strongest arguments are those that emerge from evidence. To guide students through this process of brainstorming ideas, collecting evidence, and shaping claims according to that evidence, I use the graphic organizer given in Table A.C.1 (a reproducible graphic organizer is also available in Appendix B).

These questions and prompts help students generate argument writing topics that are relevant to them and that are based on the evidence they've found in their research. In a recent professional development workshop I conducted, a teacher asked me for argument writing topics to give his students. I explained to him that the students would be more motivated— and likely do stronger work—if they explored and ultimately arrived at topics using a process like the one this graphic organizer facilitates. "Help your students create their own topics," I told this teacher. "Teach them how to generate ideas for a topic and how to connect claims and evidence. Then let them go for it. They'll be excited, motivated, and ready to write strong argument essays!"

TABLE A.C.1 Graphic Organizer for Selecting a Topic

What Is an Issue about Which You Feel Strongly?	Why Do You Feel Strongly about That Issue?	What Argument Would You Make about This Issue?	What Are Some Highlights from the Evidence You Found Related to This Issue?	Based on This Evidence, What Claim Will You Make in Your Argument Essay?

Annotated Bibliography

Excerpts from Argument Essays Featured in This Book, Aligned with Specific Common Core Standards

This annotated bibliography contains the following information: 1) The titles of the argument essays that I describe in this book as exemplars of the tools of argument informational writing (these essays are pieces I wrote to show my middle school students examples of effective argument writing), 2) A tool of argument writing found in each work, 3) The Common Core Writing Standards associated with that tool, 4) An excerpt from that work, found earlier in this book, that demonstrates exactly how the piece contains that argument writing tool, and 5) Information on which chapter in this book the concept is discussed (in case you want to refer back to the text for more information on a concept).

The annotated bibliography is designed to make this book as user-friendly as possible. It is organized alphabetically by essay title and each entry includes important details designed to help you use these works to teach your students about the tools of argument writing.

Essay Title: "Don't Trust Amazon.com's Customer Reviews"
Featured Argument Writing Tool: Introducing claims
Related Common Core Standards: W.6.1.A, W.7.1.A, W.8.1.A
Excerpt That Demonstrates Concept:

"What do you most enjoy about the internet? Some people like the way the internet gives everyone a voice—anyone with internet access can express his or her opinion about anything. There are many ways people can share their opinions online: they can create their own websites and express their thoughts on social networking sites like Facebook and Twitter. In addition, people can share their thoughts by posting product reviews on websites like Amazon.com that sell these items. Amazon.com sells a wide range of objects, and the majority of items for sale on this website have been reviewed by someone. Reviewers rate items by giving between one and five stars and can write a description of their thoughts on the item to go along with this rating. Prospective buyers should not trust these online reviews when making their purchases. Instead, consumers should rely on expert opinions and credible sources when making purchases."

Discussed in Chapter: 1

Another Featured Argument Writing Tool in This Essay: Supporting claims with reasons and evidence while using credible sources
Related Common Core Standards: W.6.1.B, W.7.1.B, W.8.1.B
Excerpt That Demonstrates Concept:

"Online reviews may be written by very biased sources. A 2013 *New York Times* article described an investigation by New York law-enforcement agents of companies that create fake online reviews and businesses that hire these companies to do so (Streitfeld, 2013). This article, titled 'Giving yourself 5 stars? Online, it might cost you,' explains that some businesses have been paying so-called 'reputa-tion' companies to write positive online reviews of their products—regardless of whether or not these reviews are accurate. The article quotes Eric Schneidermann, the New York Attorney General, who argues that fake online reviews are especially dishonest: 'When you look at a billboard, you can tell it's a paid advertisement—but on Yelp or Citysearch, you assume you're reading authentic con-sumer opinions, making this practice even more deceiving.' Fake online reviews have become so problematic and widespread that researchers from Cornell University have developed a computer program designed to detect dishonest reviews (Ott, Choi, Cardie, & Hancock, 2011). The combination of the New York investigation and the need for the Cornell computer program strongly suggests that online reviews have the strong possibility of being untrustworthy."

Discussed in Chapter: 3

Another Featured Argument Writing Tool in This Essay: Using words, phrases, and clauses to create cohesion and clarify relationships
Related Common Core Standards: W.6.1.C, W.7.1.C, W.8.1.C
Excerpt That Demonstrates Concept:

"People who hold this belief might feel that it is useful to read comments from anyone who wants to review an item, regardless of that person's qualifications. Despite these widespread beliefs, this availability to the general public is precisely the problem with online reviews; when all people can review items, there is no guarantee that the reviewers will be knowledgeable about a product and present an unbiased opinion."

Discussed in Chapter: 5

Another Featured Argument Writing Tool in This Essay: Creating an effective concluding section
Related Common Core Standards: W.6.1.E, W.7.1.E, W.8.1.E
Excerpt That Demonstrates Concept:

"If you want to know the most accurate and unbiased information about products you're interested in purchasing, pay attention to unbiased expert reviews published in reputable newspapers and magazines. Untrustworthy reviews on websites like Amazon.com have become a major problem for consumers, who can no longer be sure if they are reading the opinion of another honest customer or someone hired by a company to make a product look good and increase its sales. The problem of potentially dishonest internet reviews is a new issue in our society; before the widespread use of online communication, we did not have so many places to find out information. Now that we do, we must be very careful about what sources we trust."

Discussed in Chapter: 7

Essay Title: "Keep Gym Class in Schools"
Featured Argument Writing Tool: Introducing claims
Related Common Core Standards: W.6.1.A, W.7.1.A, W.8.1.A
Excerpt That Demonstrates Concept:

"The people in charge of our schools make a lot of tough decisions. Politicians, school board members, and policy makers have to think about issues like what books should be taught, whether or not schools should have dress codes, and how much time students should spend on different activities. Deciding how much time students should spend on different activities can be especially difficult. With new, challenging standards like the Common Core State Standards being used in schools and limited amounts of money, some schools have cut or reduced "specials" like gym class. These administrators should keep gym class in schools. Gym is a valuable part of the school experience that increases students' chances to live happy, successful lives and should not be eliminated."

Discussed in Chapter: 1

Another Featured Argument Writing Tool in This Essay: Supporting claims with reasons and evidence while using credible sources
Related Common Core Standards: W.6.1.B, W.7.1.B, W.8.1.B
Excerpt That Demonstrates Concept:

"One of the many ways gym classes benefit students is that, according to recent research, students who are physically fit perform better academically. A study published in *The Journal of Pediatrics* examined the aerobic fitness and reading and math test scores of almost 12,000 elementary and middle school students in Nebraska; the researchers found that aerobically fit students were more likely than aerobically unfit students to pass the state's reading and math tests. According to the study's authors, "to improve academic performance, schools should focus on the aerobic fitness of every student" (Rauner, Walters, Avery, & Wanser, 2013, p. 344). This study's results clearly reveal a benefit of gym classes: fit students are more likely to succeed academically."

Discussed in Chapter: 3

Another Featured Argument Writing Tool in This Essay: Creating an effective concluding section
Related Common Core Standards: W.6.1.E, W.7.1.E, W.8.1.E
Excerpt That Demonstrates Concept:

"Gym class is an important part of the school curriculum that, according to research, helps maximize student success. In today's high-stakes-testing environment and increasingly innovative world, our students need as much support as possible. Keeping gym class in school is an opportunity to help students achieve high academic goals while also contributing to the health of our country's youth. These academic and health benefits can positively impact our society in a number of ways, ranging from more students attending college to fewer health problems among children. So, if anyone ever asks if you believe gym class is important, say 'Yes! It keeps our young people fit and intelligent—a great combination!'"

Discussed in Chapter: 7

Essay Title: "Lower the Cost of College"
Featured Argument Writing Tool: Introducing claims

Related Common Core Standards: W.6.1.A, W.7.1.A, W.8.1.A
Excerpt That Demonstrates Concept:

"Each year, millions of young people enroll in America's colleges. Excited by the opportunities of college and optimistic about their futures, these students frequently see college as a step toward realizing their dreams. Some may dream of being teachers, others might hope to be doctors, and some might even think about being the President of the United States. College is often thought of as a time to explore new ideas by taking interesting classes, joining exciting groups, and making new friends. However, the high price of college is impacting many students' futures: the money that students need to borrow in order to attend college is limiting their opportunities after it. College needs to cost less in order to help more young people achieve their goals."

Discussed in Chapter: 1

Another Featured Argument Writing Tool in This Essay: Supporting claims with reasons and evidence while using credible sources
Related Common Core Standards: W.6.1.B, W.7.1.B, W.8.1.B
Excerpt That Demonstrates Concept:

"The high costs of college are making it difficult for young college graduates to live independently. An educational research organization called The Institute for College Access and Success (TICAS) explains that two-thirds of American college graduates graduate in debt from student loans, and the average borrower will owe $26,600 in these loans (TICAS, 2013). One effect of these student loans is that more recent college graduates are living with their parents than ever before (Weissman, 2013). In an article in *The Atlantic* magazine, author Jordan Weissman explains that '61 percent more college-educated 18–34-year-olds were living with their families in 2011 than in 2001.' Lauren Asher, the president of TICAS says in an article in *Forbes* magazine that the increased student debt faced by recent graduates results in them needing to delay their independence: 'Debt costs you time in savings, pushes back when and whether you can buy a home, start a family, open a small business or access capital' (Denhart, 2013)."

Discussed in Chapter: 3

Another Featured Argument Writing Tool in This Essay: Using words, phrases, and clauses to create cohesion and clarify relationships
Related Common Core Standards: W.6.1.C, W.7.1.C, W.8.1.C
Excerpt that Demonstrates Concept:

"College is often thought of as a time to explore new ideas by taking interesting classes, joining exciting groups, and making new friends. However, the high price of college is impacting many students' futures: the money that students need to borrow in order to attend college is limiting their opportunities after it."

Discussed in Chapter: 5

Another Featured Argument Writing Tool in This Essay: Establishing and maintaining a formal style
Related Common Core Standards: W.6.1.D, W.7.1.D, W.8.1.D
Excerpt That Demonstrates Concept:

"Some people oppose efforts to decrease college costs, asserting that making colleges cheaper for students will require the government to spend money to offset the lower tuition amounts that the colleges receive and that the government cannot afford to do so. While the government may need to spend money for college costs to decrease, there are a number of ways that having a highly educated and debt-free population can positively impact society. Young people in a great deal of debt can't purchase many things, which hurts the economy. If recent college graduates are concerned with paying off their loans and not purchasing houses and cars, the housing and auto industries may decline. However, these and other businesses may thrive if young people are not overcome with debt. Also, a country with more well-educated people contains more individuals who can produce innovations, ideas, and products that can bring profit to the country's industries and create jobs. If the government invests in helping students graduate debt-free from college, these promising possibilities may become reality."

Discussed in Chapter: 6

Essay Title: "The Importance of Baseball"
Featured Argument Writing Tool: Acknowledging alternate or opposing claims

Related Common Core Standards: W.7.1.A, W.8.1.A
Excerpt That Demonstrates Concept:

"Some detractors of baseball say that the game only remains popular and important among specific segments of the population, such as older people who enjoy a slower-paced sport or individuals in particular places where the game is disproportionately popular. Still others may contend that baseball's time has simply passed. These individuals may say that, while the sport was once thought of as our nation's pastime, it is no longer very popular or relevant, because it doesn't deliver a great deal of high-speed action like football, basketball, and automobile racing do. They may claim that we live in an age when people want high-speed, action-packed entertainment, and baseball is not relevant in a society that values these characteristics."

Discussed in Chapter: 2

Another Featured Argument Writing Tool in This Essay: Organizing reasons and evidence logically
Related Common Core Standards: W.6.1.A, W.7.1.A, W.8.1.A
Excerpt That Demonstrates Concept:

"One indicator of baseball's importance is its global popularity. Although it has been traditionally called America's 'National Pastime,' baseball has been embraced by athletes in countries around the world. One example of this is the World Baseball Classic, a tournament in which countries from all over the globe compete. The World Baseball Classic has grown so much in popularity around the world that event organizers increased the amount of competing countries from 16 in 2009 to 28 in 2013 (MLB, 2011). In addition, games of the 2013 World Baseball Classic were played in four different countries: Japan, Puerto Rico, Taiwan, and the United States of America (Sports Illustrated for Kids, 2013). The World Baseball Classic is a key representation of baseball's global appeal."

Discussed in Chapter: 4

Another Featured Argument Writing Tool in This Essay: Using words, phrases, and clauses to create cohesion and clarify relationships
Related Common Core Standards: W.6.1.C, W.7.1.C, W.8.1.C

Excerpt That Demonstrates Concept:

"The World Baseball Classic has grown so much in popularity around the world that event organizers increased the amount of competing countries from 16 in 2009 to 28 in 2013 (MLB, 2011). In addition, games of the 2013 World Baseball Classic were played in four different countries: Japan, Puerto Rico, Taiwan, and the United States of America (Sports Illustrated for Kids, 2013)."

Discussed in Chapter: 5

Essay Title: "Introverts Can Be Great Leaders, Too"
Featured Argument Writing Tool: Acknowledging alternate or opposing claims
Related Common Core Standards: W.7.1.A, W.8.1.A
Excerpt That Demonstrates Concept:

"Some may claim that outgoing and extroverted people are best suited to leadership because extroverts can use their verbal skills to inspire others. However, a leader can inspire others in a variety of ways, not just through oral language. Leaders' actions and achievements can be just as inspirational as motivational speeches. Other people feel that introverts and extroverts can both be leaders in some situations, but specific situations call for extroverted leaders. Despite this belief that some hold, just as there are a variety of ways to inspire others, there are a variety of ways to lead in all situations. While some situations might be most commonly associated with vocal leaders, that doesn't mean extroverts can't be equally successful in them. Successful sports coaches have a range of personalities and styles, from vocal to quiet, contemplative personas. Similarly, research on effective teachers shows that individuals with a wide range of personalities can become strong teachers that successfully engage and lead their students through learning activities (Wiens & Ruday, 2014)."

Discussed in Chapter: 2

Another Featured Argument Writing Tool in This Essay: Organizing reasons and evidence logically
Related Common Core Standards: W.6.1.A, W.7.1.A, W.8.1.A

Excerpts That Demonstrate Concept:

"Many effective leaders throughout history have been introverts. Jennifer Kahnweiler, in her 2009 book *The Introverted Leader*, identifies famous executives and leaders such as Bill Gates, Mother Theresa, and Abraham Lincoln as naturally introverted. In many ways, explains Kahnweiler, these leaders may have actually been helped by being introverted, as introverts are especially good at thinking and processing their ideas before acting. The introverted nature of these people shows that introverts have held leadership roles for a long time and suggests that they will continue to do so in the future."

"Not only can introverts and extroverts both be effective leaders, but research published in 2010 in the *Harvard Business Review* explains that, when employees of a company are proactive and offer ideas to improve the company, introverted leaders are more effective than extroverted ones (Grant, Gino, & Hofman, 2010). The introverted leaders described in the study 'listened carefully and made employees feel valued, motivating them to work hard.' The authors of this study explain that 'it's worth reexamining that stereotype' that effective leaders are always extroverts, as there are many situations where this is not the case."

Discussed in Chapter: 4

Essay Title: "Schools Should Stay Away from Computer Grading"
Featured Argument Writing Tool: Introducing claims
Related Common Core Standards: W.6.1.A, W.7.1.A, W.8.1.A
Excerpt That Demonstrates Concept:

"How are computers used in your school? They might be used by students for typing papers, creating presentations, and doing research. They might be used by teachers for taking attendance, recording students' grades, and emailing administrators. A hot topic in education today is the idea that computer programs can grade students' writing. Software developers have recently created programs that can grade students' papers, creating a situation in which teachers no longer grade their students' works. These programs have been adopted in several colleges and even some middle and high schools. Even though computer programs that grade student writing are gaining popularity, schools should stay away from them. Computer grading does not provide students with important benefits that teacher grading does."

Discussed in Chapter: 1

Another Featured Argument Writing Tool in This Essay: Supporting claims with reasons and evidence while using credible sources
Related Common Core Standards: W.6.1.B, W.7.1.B, W.8.1.B
Excerpt That Demonstrates Concept:

"A careful look at the evidence about computer grading shows that grading programs are not very reliable methods of evaluating student writing. According to a news report by Molly Bloom of NPR, Les Perelman, director of the writing center at MIT, experimented with a computer grading program and found a number of inaccuracies (Bloom, 2012). For example, when Perelman wrote a sample essay that was graded by a computer grading program, he noted that the program identified some sections of the essay as incorrect that were actually correct and didn't notice some punctuation mistakes that Perelman intentionally included. Perelman summarized the accuracy of the computer grading program by explaining, 'In other words, it doesn't work very well.'"

Discussed in Chapter: 3

Another Featured Argument Writing Tool in This Essay: Using words, phrases, and clauses to create cohesion and clarify relationships
Related Common Core Standards: W.6.1.C, W.7.1.C, W.8.1.C
Excerpt That Demonstrates Concept:

"According to a news report by Molly Bloom of NPR, Les Perelman, director of the writing center at MIT, experimented with a computer grading program and found a number of inaccuracies (Bloom, 2012). For example, when Perelman wrote a sample essay that was graded by a computer grading program, he noted that the program identified some sections of the essay as incorrect that were actually correct and didn't notice some punctuation mistakes that Perelman intentionally included."

Discussed in Chapter: 5

Another Featured Argument Writing Tool in This Essay: Creating an effective concluding section
Related Common Core Standards: W.6.1.E, W.7.1.E, W.8.1.E
Excerpt That Demonstrates Concept:

"Computer grading has become a popular trend in some circles, but research studies and expert opinions on writing assessment strongly advise against it. Since today's schools value rigorous standards and assessments, it is especially important that students receive accurate, high-quality feedback from teachers who know them well and are familiar with their works—features that are best provided by human grading. The conflict between human vs. computer grading raises an intriguing question with great relevance to life today—Is it better to choose a new technique because it is faster and technology-based, or is it better to choose a technique that isn't as fast but is significantly more effective? Computer grading is appealing to some because it is faster and tech-oriented, but it certainly is not the best choice for our schools and students."

Discussed in Chapter: 7

Essay Title: "Smaller Classes, Successful Students"
Featured Argument Writing Tool: Acknowledging alternate or opposing claims
Related Common Core Standards: W.7.1.A, W.8.1.A
Excerpt That Demonstrates Concept:

"There are those who believe that schools should not prioritize keeping class sizes small. Those people might say that schools are very expensive to operate and that having more students in a class allows the school to save money and avoid further cutting budgets. Schools could then use the money they save to pay for things like books, technology, sports equipment, and other items that can enhance students' school experiences. Others say that having more students in a class doesn't necessarily impact how much students learn in a particular class."

Discussed in Chapter: 2

Another Featured Argument Writing Tool in This Essay: Organizing reasons and evidence logically
Related Common Core Standards: W.6.1.A, W.7.1.A, W.8.1.A
Excerpts that Demonstrate Concept:

"Research suggests that students in small classes can maximize students' chances of being successful later in life. For example, a study published in Columbia University's *Teachers College Record* in 2001 called 'The Enduring Effects of Small Classes' states that students who are in small classes in early grades are more likely than students in larger classes to get higher grades, score better on standardized tests, graduate from high school, and go to college (Finn, Gerber, Achilles, & Boyd-Zaharias, 2001). The findings of this study make a compelling case for keeping class sizes small, as the increased chances of these long-term successes are important for not only our students but society as a whole."

"In addition, smaller class sizes can reduce the number of teachers leaving their professions. The National Commission on Teaching and America's Future reported in 2007 that close to 50 percent of new teachers leave teaching within five years, and a 2002 New York City Department of Education report stated that excessive class size was a major reason teachers left their jobs after only one year (Gallagher, 2002). If schools can maintain smaller class sizes, they can eliminate this significant reason for teachers leaving their jobs, providing schools with continuity and reducing the constant need for schools to train and develop novice teachers."

Discussed in Chapter: 4

Another Featured Argument Writing Tool in This Essay: Using words, phrases, and clauses to create cohesion and clarify relationships
Related Common Core Standards: W.6.1.C, W.7.1.C, W.8.1.C
Excerpt That Demonstrates Concept:

"Walk into a classroom in a public school, and you are likely to see dedicated teachers and hard-working students. However, you are also likely to see more students crammed into each classroom than ever before. The large amount of students in each classroom is an important issue in 21st century schools: according to a 2011 *New York Times* article titled 'Tight Budgets Mean Squeeze in Classrooms,' funding cuts and teacher layoffs have led to increasingly more students in public school classes (Dillon, 2011). For example, this article states that a proposal in Detroit would increase high school classes to 60 students. It is imperative that schools reverse this trend and ensure small classes for their students. Small classes can maximize their students' chances of success."

Discussed in Chapter: 5

References

Abbott, J. (2000). "Blinking out" and "Having the touch": Two fifth-grade boys talk about flow experiences in writing. *Written Communication, 17* (1), 53–92.

Atwell, N. (1998). *In the middle: New understandings about writing, reading, and learning.* Portsmouth, NH: Heinemann.

Bloom, M. (2012). Computers grade essays fast, but not always well. *National Public Radio.* Retrieved from: www.npr.org/2012/06/07/154452475/computers-grade-essays-fast-but-not-always-well.

Bratcher, S., & Ryan, L. (2004). *Evaluating children's writing: A handbook of grading choices for classroom teachers* (2nd ed.). Mahwah, NJ: Lawrence Erlbaum.

Burns, K. (Director). (1994). *Baseball* [Documentary film]. United States: Florentine Films.

Centers for Disease Control. (2014). Childhood obesity facts. Retrieved from: www.cdc.gov/healthyyouth/obesity/facts.htm.

Common Core State Standards Initiative. (2010). Common core state standards for English language arts. Retrieved from: www.corestandards.org/ELA-Literacy.

Denhart, C. (2013). How the $1.2 trillion college debt crisis is crippling students, parents, and the economy. *Forbes.* Retrieved from: www.forbes.com/sites/specialfeatures/2013/08/07/how-the-college-debt-is-crippling-students-parents-and-the-economy.

Dillon, S. (2011). Tight budgets mean squeeze in classrooms. *The New York Times.* Retrieved from: www.nytimes.com/2011/03/07/education/07classrooms.html?pagewanted=1.

Ehmann, S., & Gayer, K. (2009). *I can write like that! A guide to mentor texts and craft studies for writers' workshop, K-6.* Newark, DE: International Reading Association.

Finn, F.B., Gerber, S.B., Achilles, C.M., & Boyd-Zaharias, J. (2001). The enduring effects of small classes. *Teachers College Record, 103* (2), 145–183.

Fisher, D., & Frey, N. (2003). Writing instruction for struggling adolescent readers: A gradual release model. *Journal of Adolescent and Adult Literacy, 46* (5), 396–407.

Fisher D., & Frey, N. (2013). A range of writing across the content areas. *The Reading Teacher, 67* (2), 96–101.

Flavell, J.H. (1979). Metacognition and cognitive monitoring. *American Psychologist, 34*, 906–911.

Fletcher, R., & Portalupi, J. (2001). *Writing workshop: The essential guide.* Portsmouth, NH: Heinemann.

Gallagher, K. (2014). Making the most of mentor texts. *Educational Leadership, 71* (7), 28–33.

Gallagher, L.P. (2002). Class size and teacher migration, 1995–2000. *Technical Appendix of the Capstone Report, Part C.* New York: New York City Department of Education.

Graham, S., & Perin, D. (2007). *Writing next: Effective strategies to improve the writing of adolescents in middle and high schools.* Washington, DC: Alliance for Excellent Education.

Grant, A., Gino, F., & Hofman, D.A. (2010). The hidden advantages of quiet bosses. *Harvard Business Review.* Retrieved from: https://hbr.org/2010/12/the-hidden-advantages-of-quiet-bosses.

Hillocks, G. (2010). Teaching argument for critical thinking and writing: An introduction. *English Journal, 99* (6), 24–32.

Kahnweiler, J.B. (2009). *The introverted leader.* San Francisco, CA: Berrett-Koehler Publishers.

Killgallon, D., & Killgallon, J. (2013). *Paragraphs for middle school: A sentence-composing approach.* Portsmouth, NH: Heinemann.

Knoester, M. (2009). Inquiry into urban adolescent independent reading habits: Can Gee's theory of discourses provide insight? *Journal of Adolescent and Adult Literacy, 52* (8), 676–685.

Kolln, M., & Funk, R. (2009). *Understanding English grammar* (8th ed.) New York: Pearson.

Ladson-Billings, G. (1995). But that's just good teaching! The case for culturally relevant pedagogy. *Theory into Practice, 34* (3), 159–165.

Lunsford, A., & Ruszkiewicz, J. (2012). *Everything's an argument* (6th ed.). Boston, MA: Bedford/St. Martins.

Markoff, J. (2013). Easy grading software offers professors a break. *The New York Times.* Retrieved from: www.nytimes.com/2013/04/05/science/new-test-for-computers-grading-essays-at-college-level.html.

MLB (Major League Baseball). (2011). 2013 World Baseball Classic field expands to 28 teams. Retrieved from: mlb.mlb.com/news/press_releases/press_release.jsp?ymd=20110601&content_id=19867334&vkey=pr_mlb&fext=.jsp&c_id=mlb.

MLB (Major League Baseball). (2014a). MLB records seventh best attendance total ever in 2014. Retrieved from: m.mlb.com/news/article/96990912/mlb-records-seventh-best-attendance-total-ever-in-2014.

MLB (Major League Baseball). (2014b). 2014 opening day rosters feature 224 players born outside the U.S. Retrieved from: m.mlb.com/news/article/70623418/2014-opening-day-rosters-feature-224-players-born-outside-the-us.

Moss, B. (2014). Teaching argument: Resources for teachers. *Voices from the Middle, 21* (3), 61–63.

National Commission on Teaching and America's Future. (2007). *The high cost of teacher turnover.* Retrieved from: http://nctaf.org/wp-content/uploads/2012/01/NCTAF-Cost-of-Teacher-Turnover-2007-policy-brief.pdf.

NCTE (National Council of Teachers of English). (2008). *Writing now: A policy research brief.* Retrieved from: www.ncte.org/library/NCTEFiles/Resources/Journals/CC/0181-sept2008/CC0181Policy.pdf.

Ott, M., Choi, Y., Cardie, C., & Hancock, J.T. (2011). Finding deceptive opinion spam by any stretch of the imagination. *Proceedings of the 49th Annual Meeting of the Association for Computational Linguistics,* 309–319.

Pearson, P.D., & Gallagher, M.C. (1983). The instruction of reading comprehension. *Contemporary Educational Psychology, 8,* 317–344.

Perelman, C., & Olbrechts-Tyteca, L. (1969). *The new rhetoric: Treatise on argumentation.* (J. Wilkinson & P. Weaver, Trans.). Notre Dame, IN: University of Notre Dame Press.

Ramage, J.D., Bean, J.C., & Johnson, J. (2010). *Writing arguments: A rhetoric with readings* (8th ed.). New York: Pearson.

Rauner, R., Walters, R., Avery, M., & Wanser, T. (2013). Evidence that aerobic fitness is more salient than weight status in predicting standardized math and reading outcomes in fourth- through eighth-grade students. *The Journal of Pediatrics, 163* (2), 344–348.

Ray, K.W. (1999). *Wondrous words: Writers and writing in the elementary classroom.* Urbana, IL: National Council of Teachers of English.

Robb, L. (2010). *Teaching middle school writers: What every English teacher needs to know.* Portsmouth, NH: Heinemann.

Sports Illustrated for Kids. (2013). Everything you wanted to know about the World Baseball Classic in one infographic. Retrieved from: sikids.com/blogs/2013/03/01/everything-you-need-to-know-about-the-world-baseball-classic-in-one-infographic.

Steinberg, M.A., & McCray, E.D. (2012). Listening to their voices: Middle schoolers' perspectives of life in middle school. *The Qualitative Report, 17,* 1–14.

Streitfeld, D. (2013). Giving yourself 5 stars? Online, it might cost you. *The New York Times.* Retrieved from: www.nytimes.com/2013/09/23/technology/give-yourself-4-stars-online-it-might-cost-you.html.

TICAS (The Institute for College Access and Success). (2013). The project on student debt. Retrieved from: www.projectonstudentdebt.org.

Weissmann, J. (2013). Here's exactly how many college graduates live back at home. *The Atlantic.* Retrieved from: www.theatlantic.com/business/archive/2013/02/heres-exactly-how-many-college-graduates-live-back-at-home/273529/.

Wheeler, R., & Swords, R. (2006). *Code switching: Teaching standard English in urban classrooms.* Urbana, IL: National Council of Teachers of English.

Wiens, P. & Ruday, S. (2014). Personality and pre-service teachers: Does it change? Does it matter? *Issues in Teacher Education, 22* (2), 7–27.

Wood, N.V. (2009). *Essentials of Argument.* Upper Saddle River, NJ: Pearson Prentice Hall.

Zinsser. W. (2006). *On writing well: 30th anniversary edition.* New York: Harper Perennial.

DATE DUE

PRINTED IN U.S.A.

environmentally friendly book printed and bound in England by www.printondemand-worldwide.com

PEFC Certified

This product is
from sustainably
managed forests
and controlled
sources

PEFC™

www.pefc.org

PEFC/16-33-415

ok is made of chain-of-custody materials; FSC materials for the cover and PEFC materials for the text pages.

308 - 290715 - C0 - 254/178/10 - PB - 9781138924390